# BANFF & LAKE LOUISE
## History Explorer

## by Ernie Lakusta
### Altitude Publishing
The C...

# Publication Information

## Altitude Publishing Canada Ltd.
## The Canadian Rockies
1500 Railway Avenue
Canmore, Alberta T1W 1P6

www.altitudepublishing.com

## Canadian Cataloguing in Publication Data
Lakusta, Ernie
Banff and Lake Louise history explorer/
Ernie Lakusta
(Altitude superguide)
Includes index.
ISBN 1-55153-636-6 (pbk.)

1. Banff (Alta.)--History. 2. Louise, Lake, Region (Alta.)--History. 3. Banff (Alta.)--Guidebooks.
4. Louise, Lake, Region (Alta.)--Guidebooks.
I. Title. II. Series.
FC3699.B25L34 2003    971.23'32    C2003-
910269-6    F1079.5B25L34 2003

**Front cover:** Georgia Engelhard and guide Ernest Feuz on Mount Victoria, Banff National Park, 1931

**Back cover:** The east gate of Rocky Mountains (Banff) National Park, 1921

**Frontispiece:** Moraine Lake, Banff National Park

## Altitude GreenTree Program

Altitude Publishing will plant in Canada twice as many trees as were used in the manufacturing of this product.

## Project Development
| | |
|---|---|
| Project Manager | Scott Manktelow |
| Layout | Linda Petras |
| Editor | Peggy Lipinski |
| Index | Elizabeth Bell |

Printed and bound in Canada by Friesen Printers, Altona. Manitoba

We acknowledge the financial support of the Government of Canada through the Book Publishing Industry Development Program (BPIDP) for our publishing activities.

# Table of Contents

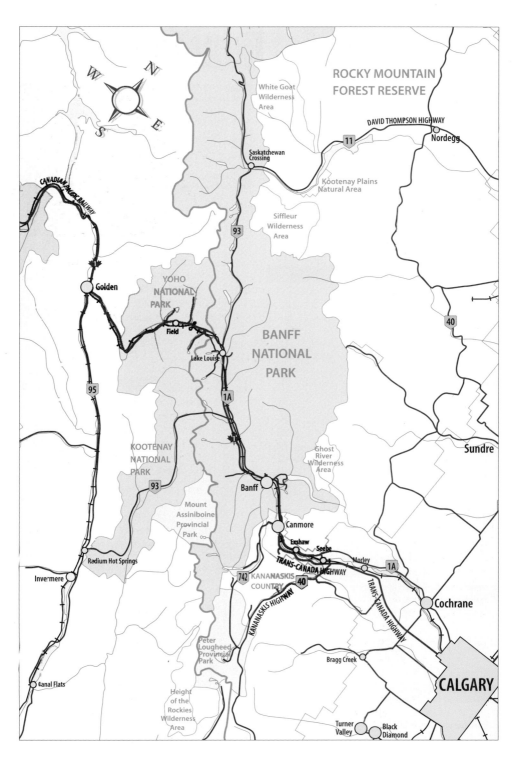

Banff National Park in the Canadian Rockies

# Introduction

The Cree called them the *Usinee Wutche* or the "Shining Mountains," while the Stoneys referred to them as the *Assin-wati*. To the early French-Canadian voyageurs they were the *montagnes des rocnes*. But gradually they became known by their English translation "Rocky Mountains," or simply, "The Rockies." Few tourists realize that their journey through the Valley of the Bow follows a path that has been used by humans for thousands of years

The written history of the region does not really begin until August 11, 1858, when Captain John Palliser, leader of the Palliser Expedition, gave a young, scholarly, athletic, and friendly individual named James Hector the following mandate: "Dr. Hector should ascend into the mountains in any direction which he thought most conducive to the interests of geological and geographical science ..." Hector chose the Bow Valley as "conducive" to their interests because, as Hector wrote, "it allowed of our entering the mountains at once without travelling further in the open country, which yields little of interest either to the geologist or the botanist.' And so, on the morning of August 11, 1858 began one of the most amazing journeys in the annals of the Canadian Rockies. Hector continued, "My party consisted of Peter Erasmus [interpreter and guide], Sutherland, and Brown, all Red River men, and also my Stone Indian friend, who had promised the previous winter to serve as my guide in the mountains ... His Indian name, which signifies 'The one with the thumb like a blunt arrow,' is so unpronounceable, I called him Nimrod, which name has stuck to him ever since."

Hector would be responsible for

**Bighorn ram on a ledge**

most of the initial exploration in the valley, but individuals with incredible ambitions and sometimes grandiose goals would follow. They would construct the first railway through the Canadian Rockies, discover hidden wonders, and construct lodges that would become tourist magnets.

One member of this new breed arrived in 1891. Samuel E.S. Allen was an extremely intelligent young man, full of excitement when he disembarked from the train at Field, B.C. He described his journey to Lake Louise in the following manner: "This entire region, being still unharmed by fires, possesses a charm which is not even exceeded by the more snowy Selkirks. The 29 km [18 miles] of increasing grandeur which I covered afoot from Field across the summit to Laggan culminated in the fitting climax of Lake Louise." Later he would convince his colleague from Yale University, Walter Wilcox, to join him and together they would begin a new chapter in exploration and discovery around Lake Louise.

These individuals left a rich legacy in their written accounts of their journeys. You can follow them in this *SuperGuide* and experience some of their feelings, emotions and sensations. Welcome to the *Usinee Wutche*.

# People of the Shining Mountains

*In the olden days some of the neighbouring tribes called us the 'People of the Shining Mountains.' These mountains are our temples, our sanctuaries, and our resting places. They are the place of hope, a place of vision, a place of refuge, a very special place where the Great Spirit speaks with us. Therefore these mountains are our sacred places.*

Chief John Snow, 1977

Mts. Whyte (left)
and Niblock (right)

# Prehistoric Hunter-Gatherers

For most of human history the splendour of the Bow Valley Parkway, and what is now much of Banff National Park, was the domain of prehistoric peoples who were hunter-gatherers. As soon as the glaciers began to recede, plants of all types and then wildlife began to invade the denuded landscape. The prehistoric peoples who roamed the river valleys revelled in the mountain scenery and set up camps on the south-facing slopes. They left no written account of their presence. The only evidence we have of their passing is in the ancient artifacts they left at these sites, which only now archaeologists are beginning to piece together. As of 1996, 430 prehistoric sites were identified within Banff National Park. This led archaeologist Gwyn Langemann to state, "It is becoming clear that there is really no pristine wilderness, that people have been living in the park for a very long time, and have been playing a role in shaping the landscape within the parks for at least 11,000 years."

Few people realize that when they are travelling the Trans-Canada Highway they are actually following a trail that had been used for thousands of years by these hunter-gatherers.

It was during the construction of these roadways that archaeologists unearthed evidence of occupation by ancient peoples. Prehistoric sites have been uncovered on the shores of Lake Minnewanka, Vermilion

Lakes, and the lower slopes of Mts. Norquay and Edith. They left evidence of their occupation in the form of ancient stone tools, flakes from tool-making activity, fire pits, and fragments of bone from the animals they butchered. Research at these sites indicates a picture of consistent use through the centuries.

Perhaps 3,000 years ago, a group of people known as the Shuswap, a tribe belonging to the interior Salish, migrated from the west and built their distinctive "pit houses" on the lower benches of Tunnel Mtn., in the region of what is now the Banff Springs Golf Course. The remains of at least 14 such dwellings have been identified at this site. Similar pit houses have been discovered in at least six other locations along the Bow River Valley in Banff National Park.

# New Arrivals

Whether or not these prehistoric peoples were the ancestors of the native peoples who came to occupy these mountains, we can only speculate. The Salish, Snake, and Kootenay frequently travelled through the mountain passes in order to reach the plains where they traded their goods and hunted buffalo.

It is evident that the Kootenay came to know the mountains and the passes intimately and they eventually became the dominant tribe in the Banff and Lake Minnewanka regions. By the late 1790s, the Kootenay had been decimated by smallpox and driven permanently across the Great Divide by the fierce Peigan. The void they created would soon be filled by a peaceful but powerful people derived from the Assiniboine Nation.

*Mt. Temple reflects in Herbert Lake*

# The Stoneys:
# People Who Cook With Stones

**Samson Beaver and his family**

Noted historian Jack Dempsey surmises that the Stoneys, also known as the Assiniboine, are part of the much larger Sioux nation from whom they separated sometime before 1640. Tradition holds that they had been living near the headwaters of the Mississippi River when they separated from the Sioux and migrated westward across the Great Plains to the foot of the Rocky Mountains.

Alexander Henry the Younger encountered the Stoneys in 1811 and described them as proficient hunters who were "the most arrant horse thieves in the world, [and] are at the same time the most hospitable to strangers who arrive in their camps." The Stoney name was derived from the term *Assinipwat*, or "Stone People," because of their method of us-

ing hot stones in their cooking.

By the early 1800s, the Stoneys had become the dominant tribe in the Bow Valley region and, according to E.J. Hart, by the late 1800s three distinct bands of Stoneys had evolved in Alberta; the Chiniki, Goodstoney (later known as Wesley), and the Bearspaw.

These mountains became the sacred places of the Stoneys. They always retained a close spiritual connection with their mountain surroundings. Chief John Snow, in his book entitled *These Mountains are our Sacred Places*, describes many localities in the mountains where spiritual rituals were performed. One of these occurred at "the sacred waters of the mountains," today's Banff Hot Springs. The Stoneys knew of the curative properties of these mineral waters long before they were "discovered" by the whites. The mountains were also the site of another important ritual in a Stoney's life — the vision quest, "a tradition handed down through the centuries and practised by us as a means of approaching the Great Spirit."

Mysticism and religion played an important role in the everyday life of the Stoney people. Nearby Sundance Canyon, and indeed the Sundance Range (see page 45) was named in honour of a Sun Dance festival (see page 45) celebrated each summer by the Stoneys. At the Hoodoos, the Stoneys placed "little personal sacrifices" of treasured objects to

appease an evil spirit. They also believed that a spirit so frightening that "all Indians stayed away from the water" lived in the waters of Lake Minnewanka. *Minnewanka* is the Stoney term for "Water of the Spirits."

Mun-uh-cha-ban, the Bow River

# The Legend of the Pasque Flower

As harbingers of spring, hikers eagerly anticipate the Pasque Flower as it emerges from the ground, often poking its way through late spring snow banks. The name "anemone" comes from the Greek word *anemos* meaning "wind," and many people refer to these members of the anemone family as "wind-flowers." These densely hairy plants are a welcome sign of spring and the source of an ancient native legend associated with the vision quest.

The following is adapted from *Old Man's Garden* by Annora Brown.

A young Indian boy named Wapee was ready to go through his ceremony to manhood in early spring. After the traditional purification he was sent into the high mountains in quest of a vision and for three days of fasting with nothing more than a buffalo robe for warmth. The first night was very cold

and when he wrapped the robe about himself he heard a voice say, "Thank you." Looking around he saw it came from a little white flower that his robe was protecting from the cold.

Wapee spent the next day in the company of this little flower and in the grandeur of the mountain scenery. The second night was just as cold and the flower was just as grateful for the protection from the cold. On the third night, Wapee again sheltered the little flower from the cold and the flower confided in him that he had a kind heart and that "Wisdom and a gentle heart will

The Pasque Flower, *Anemone patens*

make of you a great leader. But when you are bowed with troubles and cares, remember that on the next hilltop you will find peace and wisdom." In a vision before dawn Wapee saw that he would one day become a great medicine man to his people.

Before returning, Wapee asked the little flower for three wishes that he could ask the Great Spirit to grant the little flower. Nodding, the flower answered, "Pray that I may have the purple and blue of the distant mountains in my petals. Then grant me a small golden sun to hold close to my heart to cheer me up on dull days when the sun is hidden. Lastly, let me have a warm coat, like your robe of fur, that I may face the cold winds that blow from the melting snow and bring men comfort and the hope of warmer winds to follow." The Great Spirit granted all of these wishes and that is how the Pasque Flower with its purplish-blue petals, bright yellow centre, and hairy covering is protected from the cold when it pokes its head through the early spring snows.

# First Contact

Mt. Aylmer    Devil's Head    Black Rock Mtn.

Devil's Head and adjoining peaks as Anthony Henday might have viewed them in December 1754

David Thompson gave us the first authentic description of the Rockies in 1787 when he wrote in his journal, "The Rocky Mountains came in sight like shining white clouds on the horizon. As we proceeded, they rose in height; their immense masses of snow appeared above the clouds forming an impassable barrier, even to [an] Eagle." David Thompson may have been the first person of European extraction to provide an authentic written impression of the Rocky Mountains, but he certainly wasn't the first explorer or fur trader to view their spectacular outline. That honour may go to Anthony Henday, a convicted smuggler in his native England, who came to Rupert's Land as an employee of the Hudson's Bay Company.

## Welcome to the
### Usinee Wutche

Although there is some doubt as to the accuracy and authenticity of Anthony Henday's journals, he may have been the first European to view the Rocky Mountains on a cold, frosty day on December 24, 1754 from a hill near present-day Innisfail. If he were the first fur trader to view the *Usinee Wutche*, a Cree term for "the shining mountains," he would have been awestruck by their magnificence. In *Behold the Shining Mountains*, historian J.G. MacGregor attempted to piece together what he feels is a close approximation of a conversation Henday had with his Cree companions as he approached the Rocky Mountains. Even though Henday's original journal has been lost to antiquity and existing copies appear to have been altered, it is not hard to imagine the following conversation taking place:

> *"This way?" Henday asked his Cree brothers, pointing south, "How far do they run?" His Cree friends replied, "For weeks of travel No one could come to the end of them." "And north?" he asked, "How far?" They shrugged their shoulders and answered as if in futility, "There is no end to them." "What is beyond them?" Again they answered as if in vain, "We do not know."*

We can only speculate about such a conversation, but isn't it fitting that the story of the Rockies should begin with a legend?

Every year millions of tourists or locals from Calgary, using the Trans-Canada Highway or Highway 1A, witness this same sight as they leave the foothills and enter the *Usinee Wutche.* Travelling west they leave the foothills and are confronted with the bold outline of a continuous chain of mountains that forms the backbone of North America. Standing boldly on the horizon, forming what seems to be an almost insurmountable barrier, they inspire our imagination and beckon us to explore.

# Historic Routes Through the Rockies

When Hudson's Bay explorer Peter Fidler journeyed to the Rocky Mountains during 1792 and 1793, he was impressed with their grandeur, writing in his journal, "The Mountain [he always referred to the Rocky Mountains in the singular] appears high — awful & very grand along," and after conferring with his Kootenay guide concluded that "There is no way of Passing over these Mountains in these Latitudes except along rivers & here it is attended with great hardship & danger."

Fidler knew other explorers had attempted to cross this barrier and that the Kootenay, Shuswap, Blackfoot, and Stoneys had intimate knowledge of passageways through the Rockies. The natives had used these routes for centuries to hunt for game and to trade their goods. It is ironic that although members of the First Nations had known of these routes for centuries, history will record that these passageways were "discovered" by explorers of European descent and most were named in their honour.

## Devil's Gap Route

The preferred route into the Rocky Mountains was through the gap between Orient Point and Mt. Costigan, which became known as Devil's Gap. This gap provided easy access from Ghost River and Lake Minnewanka to the Bow River near the base of Cascade Mtn.

Perhaps it was the abundance of game in the area or the safety of this route north of the Bow River that forced visitors to choose the Devil's

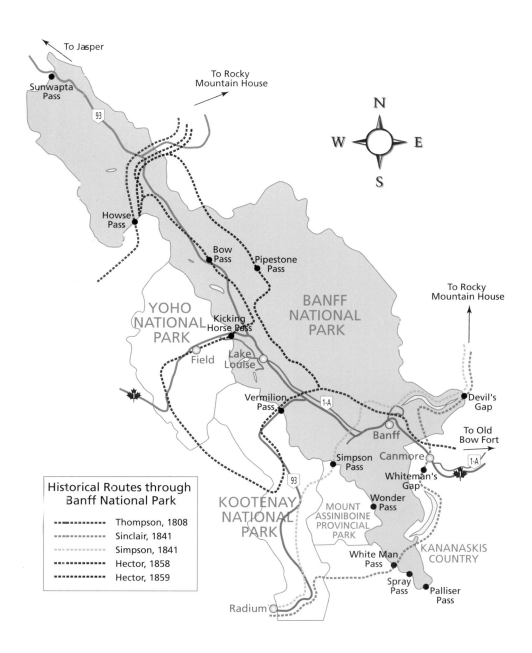

Map of Historic Routes through Banff National Park

Saddle Pk.  Orient Point  Devil's Gap  Mt. Costigan

Gap route. After all, the fierce and warlike Pagan were known to frequent the region along the Bow River and ever since David Thompson's time were not been outwardly friendly to explorers whom they felt had supplied guns to the Kootenay, their traditional enemy. Therefore, it is not unusual that, in 1841, Cree and Stoney guides led the first Europeans into the Rockies via Devil's Gap. The distinctive shapes of Orient Point and Devil's Head which were visible on the horizon for many kilometres, acted as landmarks in guiding the early visitors to the Rockies through this gap. In 1841 Sir George Simpson became the first to record using this route to enter the mountains and wrote, "The path which we had been following, was a track of the Assiniboines, carried, for the sake of concealment, through the thickest forests. These Indians and Peechee [Simpson's guide] were the only persons that had ever used this route; and we were the first whites that had attempted this pass of the mountains."

## The Bow River Valley Route

From its source high in the mountains on the Continental Divide at Bow Summit, the Bow River winds a sinuous course for over 500 km to its confluence with the Old Man River. There it becomes the South Saskatchewan River. Originally, the Stoneys knew the river by the name *Mun-uh-cha-ban* or "the place one takes bows from.' Today, they know it as *Mini-thni-Wapta* or "Cold Water River." The Peigan had a similar name, *Manachaban sipi,* meaning "where the bow reeds grow." In both cases the material used to manufacture their bows was the Douglas fir tree that grew in the Bow Valley.

David Thompson entered the valley on November 29, 1800 and recorded this in his journal:

*Our road lies along the Bow River, which all along to the very mountains has beautiful Meadows along its Banks. Those in the South Side the*

Entrance to the Rocky Mountains through Devil's Gap

Bow Lake and
Glacier, headwaters
of the Bow River

*River tho' the most extensive, are so frequently cut by Brooks, who's Banks here are always high & often very steep: and Ravelines, the remains of old Stream, whose water has failed. On the North Side the Meadows are not so extensive, but they are the best Road, as they are not so often intersected by small Streams which come pouring down from the Hills.*

Hector probably followed this same ancient trail mentioned by Thompson when he used the valley to explore the upper reaches of the Bow River in 1858–59.

# Peigan Post (Old Bow Fort)

Peigan Post was constructed in 1832 on the banks of the Bow River near the mouth of Old Fort Creek as an alternative trading post to Rocky Mountain House. The Hudson's Bay Company constructed the post in an attempt to lure the Peigan and Blackfoot away from trading their furs with the Americans. The post was constantly under danger of attack and finally, out of frustration, was abandoned in the fall of the same year.

The Hudson's Bay Company briefly reopened the post on August 10, 1833, but it was in such a state of disrepair that it was rebuilt in 1833 complete with a five-sided stockade to protect its inhabitants. The cost of defending the post was deemed too expensive and, in January 1834, Peigan Post was abandoned forever. The site was quickly vandalized and the ruins became known as Old Bow Fort.

It was an exciting day when the Palliser Expedition finally reached the site of Old Bow Fort overlooking the picturesque Bow River Valley on the afternoon of August 7, 1858. Palliser noted that all that remained of the original structure was "marked only by a group of mud and stone chimneys, the remainder of the fort having been constructed of timber, all of which was long ago removed and used by the Indians for firewood."

# The Palliser Expedition

By 1846 settlement of the disputed Oregon Territory finally brought to an end squabbling between the United States and Britain over the boundary between the United States and western British North America. In the wake of American expansionism, Britain was desperate to acquire detailed information on the possibility of expansion and settlement in the western territories, but at that time very little was known of the climate, natural resources, and agricultural potential of western British North America. Even less was known of the Rocky Mountains and whether trade routes existed through this barrier.

The Palliser Expedition was organized to investigate these inadequacies. Captain John Palliser (1817–87) was selected to head the expedition and given the following mandate:

*At the commencement of the season of 1858, you will start, as soon as the weather is sufficiently open and favourable, to explore the country between the two branches of the Saskatchewan River and south of the southern branch, and thence proceeding westward to the head of the waters of that river, you will endeavour, from the best information you can collect, to ascertain whether one or more practicable passes exist over the Rocky Mountains within the British territory, and south of that known to exist between Mount Brown and Mount Hooker.*

Palliser was the eldest son (from a family of five boys and fours girls) of a wealthy Irish landowner, Colonel Wray Palliser and his wife

Captain John Palliser and James Hector

Anne Gledstanes. He was described by his Métis guide and interpreter Peter Erasmus as being "quite tall and always appeared to hold himself erect so that he had a straight-backed military appearance," and respected not because of his rank but because "the character of the man himself and his attitude of friendly equality aroused a loyalty that was greater than mere respect. Every man was stirred to give his best to any task assigned to him."

Joining Palliser was Dr. James Hector, a 23-year-old Scot who held degrees in medicine and geology; Eugène Bourgeau, a botanist in charge of making an inventory of the flora of the region; and Lieutenant

Thomas Blakiston who would survey Rupert's Land to supplement the maps of David Thompson and Peter Fidler. John William Sullivan was appointed the expedition's astronomer and secretary and Peter Erasmus was to serve as the party's guide and translator.

# Sir James Hector (1834-1907)

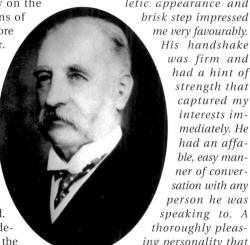

**Dr. James Hector**

Perhaps no other explorer has left their legacy on the Rocky Mountains of Banff National Park more than Sir James Hector. His stay was brief, just two years, but in those two years he recorded more information on the geography, geology, and wildlife of the region than any person past or present.

James Hector was born on March 6, 1834, in Edinburgh, Scotland. He graduated with a degree in medicine from the University of Edinburgh at the age of 23. Hector was highly recommended for the position of geologist/naturalist on the Palliser Expedition by Sir Roderick Murchison, the President of the Royal Geographical Society. On May 25, 1875, at the age of 23, Hector became the youngest member of the Palliser Expedition.

What type of man was about to partake in one of the most extraordinary journeys in the history of western Canada? We are fortunate to have a first-hand testimony as to the character of this remarkable man by Peter Erasmus, who served as guide and interpreter for the Palliser Expedition, and is one of the few men who personally knew James Hector. Erasmus recounted that he had expected:

*... a scholarly type, but his athletic appearance and brisk step impressed me very favourably. His handshake was firm and had a hint of strength that captured my interests immediately. He had an affable, easy manner of conversation with any person he was speaking to. A thoroughly pleasing personality that had nothing of that assumed superiority or condescending mannerism that I was beginning to associate with all Englishmen of my narrow acquaintance. I liked the man at once and nothing in my experience on the expedition or elsewhere ever changed this good opinion.*

How many of us would love to have such a glowing character assessment in our résumés?

It is easy to understand Hector's ability to withstand all manner of hardship he was about to endure as Erasmus continues his assessment of Hector, stating that feats of physical endurance and strength under all kinds of hardships are the:

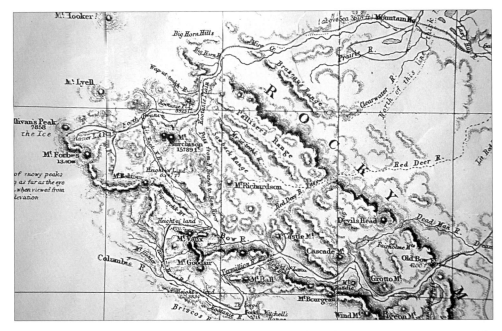

*Yardstick of a man's true worth, the same qualities that won Dr. Hector the respect and admiration of the plainsmen far beyond those that knew him personally ... He could walk, ride, or tramp on snowshoes with the best of our men, and never fell back on his position to soften his share of hardships, but in fact gloried in his physical ability after a hard day's run to share in the work of preparing camp for the night, or even helping get up wood for an all-night fire. He was admired and talked about by every man that travelled with him ...*

Hector was always willing to apply his medical knowledge and often administered to the well being of the aboriginal people he encountered. They revered his healing powers and considered him a great "medicine man," a trait that "won him admiration in many teepees that never saw the man." Yes, even at the tender age of 23, James Hector had

all the qualities required of a great leader. Many prestigious appointments in New Zealand followed his expedition exploits and he was knighted in 1887.

A lake, a gorge, a glacier, and a creek were named in his honour but most fittingly, in 1884, George Dawson named spectacular Mt. Hector to commemorate the accomplishments of this great man.

**Top: Part of the map of western Canada prepared by the Palliser Expedition showing the route taken by James Hector in 1858**

**Bottom: Mt. Hector from Kicking Horse Pass**

# Creating a National Dream

## A Spirit Rules the Hot Springs

Dan Frache's *The Chamber of Jewels,* the discovery of the cave at the Cave and Basin

*Once on the top [of] the first bench we rushed around to try and locate the place the warm water came from. This did not take long. Out of a beautiful circular basin, jammed full of logs all the way in size from four to eight inches in diameter, some ten inches, seeped this warm water. Our enthusiastic interest at this discovery was beyond the description of words ... So we moved up to another bench and to our utter astonishment we came upon a great cave 35 to 40 feet in depth. This was the greatest climax to a major discover that we had ever seen. Frank McCabe, Tom McCardell and myself just stood in silence looking at this mysterious grotto where warm water bubbled from its depths.*

William McCardell

The creation of Banff National Park closely follows the discovery and development of the mineral hot springs at the base of Sulphur Mtn. This is not to say that the whereabouts or use of these mineral springs had not been known or used by the peoples who roamed these mountains thousands of years ago. Archaeological evidence unearthed around the Vermilion Lakes area has uncovered evidence of human habitation in the Bow Valley in Banff National Park dating back at least 10,000 years. Surely over the millenia, on some crisp, cold, frosty morning, someone's curiosity would have been piqued by the steamy mist arising from the hot water coming from the slopes of Sulphur Mtn.

By the time the Stoneys had become the dominant tribe in this region centuries later, they were well aware of the mineral springs and their apparent curative properties. Chief John Snow describes localities in the mountains where spiritual rituals were performed, one of which was located at "the sacred waters of the mountains," today's hot springs. Long before European people came, these mineral springs showed some of the mysterious ways of the Creator and the Stoneys are said to have heard a "spirit" talking to them from its waters. Perhaps the singing or the whistling sound (much like the sound from the bone whistles used during the Sun Dance) they heard was the source of the ancient legend, passed down from generation to generation. They never saw the source of the singing but would say, "It is a spirit that rules the hot springs."

Ella Clark recounts a story about the springs told to her by Stoney Chief Walking Buffalo:

*The people would come and bathe in the springs because of the medicine in their waters. They would drop something in*

**Lower Banff Hot Springs**

*the water as a sacrifice, as a thank you to the spirits for the use of their water. But since the white man came, the strength has gone out of the water. That mysterious power that comes from the spirits is there no more. Probably the white people do not pray to get well the way the Indians used to pray to the spirits to cure them from their sickness. This is how the strength of the waters healed the sick.*

# The Legend of the Hot Springs

Mabel Williams suggests that the original discoverer of the hot springs was not human but an old rheumatic grizzly bear. This legend asserts that years before the construction of the railway a trapper had come across an old grizzly trail, which he followed to a pool of hot water beneath the slopes of Sulphur Mtn. It is said that the trapper even witnessed the old grizzly limping down the trail and lowering himself into the mineral waters in order to soothe his aching, arthritic bones.

Although only a tale, it is interesting to note that when William Pearce was investigating the area in 1884 he mentioned that there was "standing and in fair preservation a trapper's log hut, located on the south bank of the Bow River, about 150 yards above where the traffic bridge now stands, and in 1884 appears to have been erected upwards of 10 years previously. No owner for the log hut ever presented himself.' Could this have been the log cabin of the legendary trapper in the tale?

# Missed Opportunities

When James Hector passed through the Banff region on his second visit in 1859, he noted that "to the right of the trail I observed some warm mineral springs which deposited iron and sulphur, and seemed to escape from beds of limestone." Failing to stop long enough to investigate the source of these springs, Hector missed a glorious opportunity to make a momentous discovery, a discovery that would have to wait another 25 years.

In 1874 Joe Healy began prospecting in the Bow Valley and claims to have discovered a small stream of hot water that flowed into the Spray River. Following this stream to its source, Healy claims to have discovered the Upper Hot Springs and then the mineral springs at the Cave and Basin the following year. Was his claim fact or another fabrication from the mind of this notorious man? After all, this is the same Joseph Healy who was responsible for the construction of the infamous whiskey post, Fort Whoop-Up, and discoverer of "huge ore deposits" on the slopes of Copper Mtn! If true, Healy did not follow up on his "discovery" and no claim was ever filed.

In 1875, Peter Young and Benjamin Pease, American fur hunters from Montana, claim to have been led to the mineral springs by some Stoneys from Morleyville, thereby claiming "discovery" of the hot springs. Young thought that the springs might someday prove to be valuable and said he erected a log cabin near the springs but failed to register a claim due to a lack of money. Young later told a small but attentive audience at the log schoolhouse operated by Andrew Sibbald in Morley that "We've never seen anything like it, nothing like it. Hot water gushing right out of the mountainside!"

# These Springs are Worth a Million Dollars

By late fall of 1883, the main line of the Canadian Pacific Railway had pushed to within a few kilometres of Kicking Horse Pass when work was suspended for the winter. Frank McCabe, William McCardell, and his younger brother Thomas (who all worked for the CPR) decided to remain in the valley to prospect and set up some traplines. Perhaps on one cold, frosty morning in November these three young men did observe mist rising from the slopes of Sulphur Mtn. and, building a crude raft, crossed the Bow River to investigate the source.

Although William McCardell's description of their discovery (see page 18) is an exciting tale and the stuff of legend, McCabe's testimony before the Hot Springs Inquiry was more matter of fact and less romantic: "...we came in and saw the pond

Left: Ruins of the original McCardell cabin

Right: Statue of William Cornelius Van Horne at The Fairmont Banff Springs Hotel

and went around the pool and saw the water running down and the grass was very green and we smelt the sulphur, and we went up and saw the cave and then went home … "

McCabe's testimony hardly contains the sense of wonder and excitement conjured up by William McCardell in *Reminiscences of a Western Pioneer*. While Tom McCardell was sent to fetch a rope, William constructed a crude ladder by cutting the branches off a lodge-pole pine tree. After the ladder had been lowered through the hole at the top of the cave, William was selected to go down first. William recounted:

*I shouted that I had reached the bottom alright, and that as soon as I had accustomed my sight to the darkness of the cavern, I would call to them at the top. This was the grandest sensation I had ever experienced in all my life … I scrambled around the edge of the water*

**William McCardell**

*and I began now to witness one of the grandest spectacles, which I believed very few men had ever beheld. Beautiful stalactites hung in great clusters from the roof of the great amphitheatre-like cavern …*

To protect their "property," they set to building a fence around it and then erected a crude log cabin near the entrance to the cave. However, they couldn't lay claim to their "discovery" because, at the time, the government of Canada did not recognize hot springs as a mineral resource.

Two years later, in the summer of 1885, Tom McCabe and Frank McCardell were paid an unexpected visit by none other than William Cornelius Van Horne, the head of the Canadian Pacific Railway. They fastened a rope around their guest for protection, and Van Horne descended their crude ladder into the bowels of the cave. Upon emerging from the depths it is said that Van Horne shouted, "These springs are worth a million dollars!" Little did McCabe and McCardell know that Van Horne meant a million dollars for the CPR and not for them.

# Creation of the Hot Springs Reserve

**NOTICE.**

# BANFF HOT SPRINGS!

The undersigned, under instructions from the the Honorable the Minister of the Interior, will be at Banff Springs on
**THURSDAY, THE 24th DAY OF JUNE, INST.,**
at 10 o'clock, A. M.,
And receive any evidence that parties may wish to offer in support of their claims as discoverers of said springs, or improvements made by them at said Springs.

All parties interested will please take notice and govern themselves accordingly.

WM. PEARCE.

Calgary. 7th June, 1886.

Left: William Pearce, the "Czar of the West"

Right: The public notice issued by William Pearce regarding claims to the Banff Hot Springs

On November 25, 1885, on the advice of William Pearce and the recommendation of the Minister of the Interior, Order-in-Council No. 2197 was passed reserving just over 26 km² on the north slopes of Sulphur Mtn., creating the Hot Springs Reserve. This Order-in-Council, signed by John J. McGee (Clerk, Privy Council), simply stated:

*His Excellency, by and with the advice of the Queen's Privy Council for Canada has been pleased to order, and it is hereby ordered, that where as near the Station of Banff on the Canadian Pacific Railway, in the Provincial District of Alberta, North West Territories,*

*there have been discovered several hot mineral springs which promise to be of great sanitary advantage to the public, and in order that proper control of the lands surrounding these springs may remain vested in the crown, the said lands in the territory including said springs and in their immediate neighbourhood, be and they are hereby reserved from sale or settlement or squatting ...*

## Legal Hassling Begins

It wasn't long before claimants to ownership of the mineral springs began to proliferate. One was D.B.

Woodworth, an influential Member of Parliament from Nova Scotia, who had duped McCabe into signing over his and the McCardells' interests for $15,000 while the McCardell brothers were away working on railway construction. The McCardells hired James Lougheed, a distinguished lawyer from Calgary, to represent their interests.

As confusion over ownership grew, it was suggested to Prime Minister John A. Macdonald that the site be set aside, controlled, and administered as a national reserve similar to a model already in existence in the United States. This meant that legal claims to the sites had to be settled and the government appointed William Pearce to head an inquiry. The matter of ownership was settled in 1886 when the inquiry recognized no claims to the springs, but did recommended compensation to the claimants for any improvements they had made at the sites. Frank McCabe and the McCardell brothers received $675 in total, while Woodworth, who hadn't paid the three CPR workers one cent of the promised money, received $1,000 as compensation for his expenditures. It is interesting to note that the original discoverers received much less than the Member of Parliament who had tried to "swindle" them out of their claim.

# Creation of Rocky Mountains National Park

On June 23, 1887, the Rocky Mountains Park Act created Canada's first national park. The Hot Springs Reserve, expanded to encompass 665 km$^2$, officially became Rocky Mountains National Park. This Act, crafted by William Pearce, included a clause that firmly established the future philosophy of Canada's National Parks stating, "The said tract of land is hereby reserved and set apart as a public park and pleasure ground for the benefit, advantage, and enjoyment of the people of Canada ..." This Act, modified to avoid the pitfalls of both the Yellowstone and Arkansas hot springs models, contained a new and surprising idea, which not only recognized that the natural beauty of the country should be included among its sources of wealth, but also included the principle that these resources belonged to all the people of the country. Canada's first national park was born.

## Growing Pains

After Canada's first national park had been created, many parliamentarians were impressed with its beauty and potential for future development and a vigorous policy for the preservation and development of all the natural resources of Canada was pursued. This desire on behalf of the government of Canada to have control of all lands designated as public reserves, and considered by some as the birth of conservationism in Canada, led to the expansion and contraction of Rocky Mountains National Park. Sir John A. Macdonald's vision of exploiting the natural resources of Canada now came head to head with the conservation policy implied in the National Parks Act. How much would be allowed and at

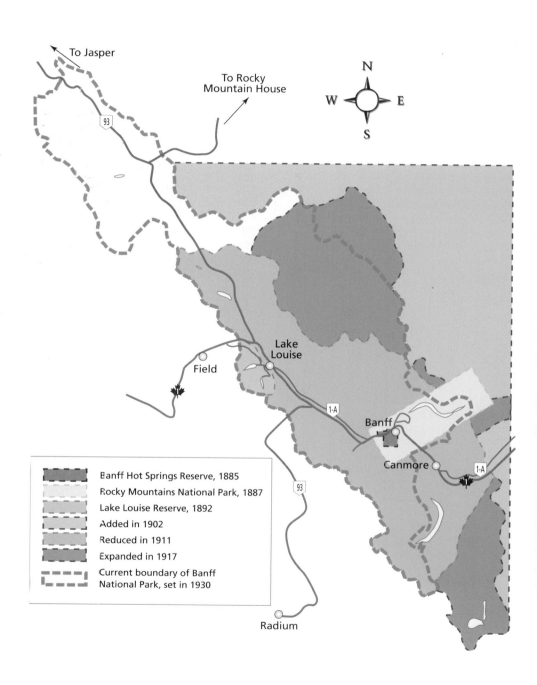

To Jasper

To Rocky Mountain House

N
W E
S

93

Lake Louise

Field

1-A

Banff

Canmore

1-A

93

Radium

Banff Hot Springs Reserve, 1885
Rocky Mountains National Park, 1887
Lake Louise Reserve, 1892
Added in 1902
Reduced in 1911
Expanded in 1917
Current boundary of Banff National Park, set in 1930

**The changing boundaries of Rocky Mountains (Banff) National Park**

what cost to the environment? Historian R. Craig Brown coined the phrase "the doctrine of usefulness" in reference to this dilemma.

In 1892 an order-in-council set aside approximately 130 km² of land designated as the Lake Louise Reserve. This reserve basically included all land that extended from the summit of the Rocky Mountains to a point about three miles east of Laggan (Lake Louise Station), then south for about six miles down the Bow Valley, and then west to the summit of the Rockies and back to its place of beginning. The Lake Louise Reserve was added to the Rocky Mountains National Park in the expansion of 1902.

In 1902 the boundaries of the park were extended dramatically to include an area of over 12,000 km² that included not only the Lake Louise Reserve but also parts of the Red Deer, Spray, and Kananaskis River systems. A forest reserve that extended as far south as the international boundary was also included under the parks administration. The administration of such a large region proved to be an impossible task and

on June 8, 1911 the Dominion Forest Reserves and Parks Act reduced the size of the park to approximately 4662 km², or by about 60 percent. Under this new Act, Rocky Mountains National Park was to be placed under the administration of a new branch of government whose first commissioner was James B. Harkin.

Once again, in 1917, the boundaries of the park were enlarged, this time to encompass most of Kananaskis Country from the Highwood Pass north (including the present-day Ghost Wilderness Area) until branching west just north of the Red Deer River to Mt. Thompson near Bow Summit.

The Cave and Basin, initial site of Banff National Park

# Banff National Park

Finally, in 1930, passage of the National Parks Act established "Banff" as the official name of the park and set out the principles by which lands within a national park were to be protected. Largely through the persistence of William Pearce and A.O. Wheeler, this Act effectively removed mining, lumber-

ing, and hydroelectric development from within park boundaries forever. This Act, and a slight adjustment in 1949, set the boundaries of Banff National Park and established its current size at 6641 km² by removing what is now Kananaskis Country, Spray Lakes, Exshaw, and Canmore from within the park boundaries.

# Death at the Gates

The eastern gates of Banff National Park in 2003

The following account was adapted from *Enchanted Banff and Lake Louise* by Frank Anderson.

Banff National Park has been relatively free of violent crime, but on the night of October 4, 1935, an event occurred in Benito, Manitoba, that would eventually lead to tragedy at the eastern park gates. On that night, four young Doukhobors (Joseph Posnikoff, John Kalmakoff, Peter Voiken, and Paul Bogarra) were all detained by Constable William Wainwright on suspicion of armed robbery. Bogarra was released for lack of evidence while the others were to be transported to jail at Pelly, Saskatchewan, some 20 miles away.

During transport the three prisoners somehow managed to overpower and then murder Constables J.G. Shaw and Wainwright. The murderers dumped the bodies of the constables in a clump of bushes outside Arran, Saskatchewan and then fled in the police car. Three days later the bodies of the missing police officers were discovered and an all-points alert was sent out for the three men.

That same evening of October 7, RCMP Constable W.E. Harrison, on RCMP patrol duty on the Banff – Calgary highway, spotted a car bearing the Manitoba licence plates heading west and notified the Banff detachment to be on the lookout. for the car. A car matching that description had just purchased gas at Exshaw and was heading towards the park gate.

Upon receiving this information, Sergeant Thomas S. Wallace, left Banff with Constables G.E. Coombe, G.C. Harrison, and G. Campbell left Banff for and went to the east gate only to learn that the suspects had refused to pay the entrance fee and had been refused entrance after failing to pay the entry fee. to the park. Park gatekeeper, Mrs. Thomas Staples, informed the officers that the suspects had turned around and were headed back to Calgary. A short distance east of the gate the officers stopped an oncoming eastbound car only to be informed that the suspects had robbed the occupants only a few minutes earlier.

Shortly thereafter a car matching the description of the suspects'

The east gate of Rocky Mountains National Park, 1921

vehicle was discovered pulled off at the side of the road. Sergeant Wallace and Constable Harrison cautiously approached the blazing headlights of the car when they were met with a blast of gunfire. In the ensuing battle both Wallace and Harrison were mortally wounded. The three suspects vanished into the bush bordering the highway.

Shortly after the battle, Constable J.H. Bonner and Magistrate Hawke from Canmore joined Constables Coombe and Campbell. Together, they set up a roadblock about five miles east of the park gate, called for more reinforcements and began a search of the woods along the roadway. Around 11:00 p.m. Constable Coombe was alerted to some rustling in the bush and in self-defence, shot and killed Joseph Posnikoff. An autopsy later determined that Posnikoff had been previously wounded three times in the battle with Wallace and Harrison.

As reinforcements arrived, the area between Canmore and the park gates was searched all night without success but then, early Tuesday morning, on October 8 the Park

Warden's office was notified that a suspect had been seen approximately six miles west of the park gate. Park Warden William Neish and Harold Leacock, another park official immediately left to investigate. When they reached the scene they were ambushed by gunfire from behind a tree stump on a hillside and dived for cover. Neish, an expert rifleman who had served with the Canadian Armed Forces, calmly fired three shots into the stump, wounding Kalmakoff twice in the abdomen and Voiken once in the lungs. Both murder suspects were rushed to Banff Springs Hospital but subsequently both died of their wounds that the same day. They were each only 21 years old.

Their deaths brought to seven the number of victims in the cross-country murder spree as both Sergeant Wallace and Constable Harrison had succumbed to their wounds and died at the Colonel Belcher Hospital in Calgary that same day. It was the bloodiest day in the history of Banff National Park.

# Gateway to the Rockies

Mt. Rundle as Hector viewed it in 1859 from Mt. Lady Macdonald

In 1858 Hector continued through "The Gap" where the Bow Valley is hemmed in by Pigeon Mtn. on the left and Grotto Mtn. to the right. He was looking up the Bow Valley towards the entrance of future Banff National Park and noted:

*Just beyond a second spur like that we were upon we had a peep into a valley so wide and extensive that it appeared to us, hemmed in as we were by precipices several thousand feet in height, that we were looking right through the range into comparatively open country. The peaks on either hand were of bold grotesque shapes, caused by the varying power of resistance which the contorted strata composing the mountains present to the atmosphere.*

Hector was glimpsing, for the time, the ancient Bow Valley hemmed in by Mt. Rundle on the left and the peaks of the Fairholme Range to the right. A sense of excitement and wonder stirred his spirit.

Since that first visit in 1858, visitors from around the world have continued to flock to Banff National Park. In a one-year period during 2001–2002, park attendance was 4,687,378 visitors. The present park gate has not always been the site of the eastern gate; it has been moved over the years in relation to the changing park boundaries. If you examine the 1921 park entrance photo on page 27, you will notice Loder Ridge in the

The Honourable Charles Stewart

Mt. Charles Stewart

Mt. Lady Macdonald

background indicating that the gate was located much farther east near the hamlet of Exshaw. Today the eastern gates are located on a bench above the Bow River between the massive 12 km-long structure of Mt. Rundle on the south and Mt. Charles Stewart to the north.

## Mt. Charles Stewart 2809 m

If you are travelling west on the Trans-Canada Highway approaching the park gate, Mt. Charles Stewart is on the right (north) side of the highway. The same peak is much more impressive when viewed travelling east in the opposite direction. The park boundary cuts right across this mountain, named after the Honourable Charles Stewart (1868–1946). Stewart was a pioneer farmer from the Killam district of Alberta who had migrated west from his birthplace in Wentworth County, Ontario. He would rise to prominence in both provincial and federal politics. As a member of the Liberal party, Stewart was first elected to the Alberta Legislature in 1909, serving as Minister of Municipal Affairs (1912–1913 and as Minister of Public Works (1913–1917). When Liberal Premier Sifton resigned to join the federal government, Stewart was appointed premier by Lieutenant-Governor Dr. Robert G. Brett (see Mt. Brett, page 63) effective October 30, 1917. In the general election of 1921, his government was defeated and he resigned as Premier of Alberta on August 13, 1917. But Stewart's political career was far from over.

Following the federal election of 1921, Stewart was invited to join the federal government where he served as Minister of the Interior. In 1922 he was elected Liberal Member of Parliament from Quebec and later in 1926 elected as Liberal Member of Parliament for Edmonton West. He continued to serve in the same ministry until 1930. In 1927 he represented Canada at the League of Nations in Geneva. The minor subsidiary peak immediately west of Mt. Charles Stewart was named Mt. Princess Margaret (2502 m) to commemorate her visit to western Canada in 1958.

Panorama from Johnson Lake

# Suppose We Call It Banff

## Arrival of the Steel Ribbon

*Banff is a place for leisure rather than the strenuous life. Pleasant drives and rides and walks abound; the river invites laziness in a canoe, and many a delightful hour may be spent amongst the lakes or threading the narrow waterways amidst the trees and bushes.*

James Outram, 1905

Sir Sandford Fleming

Whether people like to believe it or not, the town of Banff owes its existence to the Canadian Pacific Railway. Even its name reflects the birthplace of a couple of the barons of the CPR. When British Columbia was admitted to Confederation as a new province in 1871, it was promised that a railroad would connect the new province to the rest of Canada. The government of Canada placed Sir Sandford Fleming, described by fellow railroader Jason C. Easton as "Canada's foremost railway surveyor and construction engineer of the nineteenth century," in charge of surveying the line that would connect east and west.

At first, Fleming favoured a northern route across the Yellow-head Pass in Jasper through Fort Edmonton. Professor John Macoun was able to convince the directors of the newly formed Canadian Pacific Railway that a more favourable southerly route existed. It has been said that at a syndicate meeting, one of directors banged his fist on the table, announcing, "Gentlemen, we will cross the prairie and go by the Bow Pass if we can get that way." With that, the fate of the line was sealed and the southern route was chosen for the main line of the CPR.

The newly formed company then hired an American engineer who was known to have "a stellar reputation as a locating engineer on U.S. lines," to find a route through the Rockies and then through the relatively unexplored Selkirk Mtns. farther west. His name was Major A.B. Rogers, and his bad temper, abrupt manner, and use of profanity had given him a notorious reputation. Rogers' incentive for finding this elusive route was a $5000 bonus and the honour of having the pass named after him. In *Diamond Hitch*, by E.J. Hart, packer Tom Wilson recounts his first meeting with "Hell's Bells" Rogers in an amusing way: "his voluminous sideburns waved like flags in a breeze; his piercing eyes seemed to look and see everything at once ..." and "every few moments a stream of tobacco juice erupted from between his sideburns."

Once Roger's Pass had been discovered as the route through the Selkirk Range, construction of the railroad progressed at a slow and costly rate. This continued until

November 7, 1885, when the province of British Columbia was linked to the rest of Canada and the "last spike" was driven at Craigellachie, B.C., marking the completion of the CPR's transcontinental railway line.

## Tunnel Mtn. 1690 m

No, there is no tunnel in, through, or under Tunnel Mtn! To the local Stoneys the mountain was called *Tatanga*, or "Sleeping Buffalo Mountain." If you use your imagination, you can definitely make out the shape of a buffalo etched against the skyline. James Hector simply referred to this minor lump of limestone as "the big hill," which is perhaps more appropriate considering its lowly stature

How did the name Tunnel Mtn. originate? In 1882, Major Rogers, while surveying for the new CPR main line, missed Hector's route around the north end of Tunnel Mtn. Instead, he proposed a line that would pass through a half-mile tunnel to be blasted through this big hill. It would have cost the CPR mil-

lions of extra dollars and the president of the CPR, William Cornelius Van Horne, was reported to be furious at the suggestion. He ordered his engineers to "take that damned tunnel out," and quickly dispatched Charles Aeneas Shaw to find an alternate route. Shaw quickly found a route around Tunnel Mtn. by way, he said, of "a valley to the west of it joining the valley of Devil's Head Creek. So I located the line up this creek and around Tunnel Mountain to the main Bow Valley, shortening the line by a mile, avoiding two long grades, and above all eliminating the tunnel." Shaw called Rogers' plan "the most extraordinary blunder I have ever known in the way of engineering."

Rogers almost completed another blunder, equal if not larger than his proposed tunnel through the mountain. If he had had his way, Siding 29, which later became the town of Banff, would have been located east, on the other side of Tunnel Mtn. Just imagine the views if Banff had been located on the other side of the mountain; residents and

Left: "Hell's Bells" Rogers

Right: Tunnel Mtn. over the Bow River

Siding 29, ca. 1883

tourists would have to be content with staring at the eastern face of Tunnel Mtn.

## Siding 29

In 1883 construction on the transcontinental railway line for the CPR continued at a feverish pace. Track laying began in Calgary in August and reached Siding 27 (soon to be renamed Canmore) in early October. It wasn't long before the steel rails reached the foot of Cascade Mtn. where Siding 29, the 29th siding west of Medicine Hat, was laid out near the waterfall from which the mountain received its name. What a boring name! It would have to change if it were to reflect the grandeur of its setting.

# Well Banff It Shall Be

Many stories exist regarding the name change to Banff, but what is known for sure is that in 1883 the name Banff came to replace the rather nondescript name of Siding 29. Some have suggested that the Land Commissioner of the CPR was randomly using Scottish names as railroad stations constructed along its main line and that Banff just happened to be the next name on the list. This suggestion is almost as boring as the name Siding 29. So, how did the name Banff come about? A rather more dramatic account by A.V. Thomas appeared on October 27, 1939, in the *Crag and Canyon* (and reprinted in the Vancouver *Province*).

Cascade Mtn.

Mt. Aylmer

According to Thomas, Harry Sandison, a prominent Winnipeger, who had been born in Scotland at Banff, suggested to then CPR Land Commissioner John McTavish that he put forward the name "Banff" at the next meeting of the CPR hierarchy. Banff was a well-known seaport and watering place at the mouth of the Deveron River. It also happened to be the ancestral home of George Stephen and Donald Smith, prominent directors of the CPR. McTavish did as requested and, upon hearing the name of Banff:

*Donald Smith looked at Mr. Stephen and went over to him and whispered. They both seemed quite excited, and Mr. Van Horne wondered what it was all about. Donald Smith then explained that he knew Banff very well, as he had been born close to there. Then Mr. Stephen said he had been born within twelve miles of Banff, and had known ever since he*

*was a boy that it was a famous watering place. It was now Mr. Van Horne's turn to say something. "I like that name 'Banff,' he said, "It's a short, snappy name. Suppose we call it Banff." And Banff it was.*

It is not know for certain whether Van Horne jumped to his feet, pounded the table with his fist, and uttered, "Well Banff it shall be," but the story has become part of the legend of the Bow Valley.

## Moving a Town

Meanwhile, at the same time that tents and rough shacks were springing up around the newly christened town of Banff, just across the Bow River, another bustling town was beginning to take shape. It was called "National Park," a name it would keep until 1888.

The "discovery" of the hot springs on the south side of the Bow River began to change the way both politicians and the CPR hierarchy

Banff townsite and Cascade Mtn. from Sulphur Mtn.

thought of land surrounding the Hot Springs Reserve. Once the potential of the hot springs became evident to government officials, a plan for the creation of an infrastructure became an urgent need. Responsibility for developing a townsite, including roadways and bridges, fell on the shoulders of surveyor and civil engineer, George A. Stewart.

Stewart came to Banff in February 1886 and by the end of winter had surveyed and plotted the locations of two townsites, one at Lake Minnewanka and the other on the banks of the Bow River across the river from Banff. Gradually a new settlement began to grow and it soon became apparent that with the development of Dr. Brett's Sanatorium the hot springs would become the focal point of the new community. The fate of "National Park" was settled when, in June 1888, the CPR built a crude log station near the site of the present railway station and the name "Banff" went on it, allocating National Park to the archives.

## The Evolution of the Town

Governing the growth of Banff has resulted in a clash of philosophical ideas ever since the passage of the Rocky Mountains National Park Act in 1902 and its amendment, the National Parks Act in 1930. On the one hand the government was committed to adhering to a policy of protecting the wilderness and its resources, while on the other hand it was faced with the problems demanded by a burgeoning tourist industry. How much commercial development could or would be allowed in order to support this demand? How much land was to be leased for private enterprise? How long were leases to last? The government was caught in a predicament; how to abide by its own principles set down in the National Parks Act while at the same time promoting settlement.

The government was quick to show its hand. In 1886 they dispatched Dominion Land Surveyor George A. Stewart to survey a large tract of land surrounding the Hot Springs Reserve that would eventually become the town of Banff. Prime Minister Sir John A. Macdonald wanted to make the infant park a great resort and a showpiece for the Dominion of Canada. In a House of Commons debate on May 3, 1887, Macdonald stated:

*There is beautiful scenery, there are the curative properties of the water, there is a genial climate, there is prairie sport and there is mountain sport; and I have no doubt that it will become a great watering-place and that there will be a large town on the south side of the Bow River where the Government have laid out a town plot ...*

Banff was about to enter a new age of development.

# The First Entrepreneur

Brett Hospital, later known as the Sanatorium Hotel (and later called Bretton Hall)

D r. R.G. Brett (see Mt. Brett for biographical information, page 68) was one of the first to recognize and take advantage of the commercial value of the mineral springs. Early in 1886 he obtained permission to build a hospital, later to be called the Sanatorium Hotel, at the south end of the Bow River Bridge (the current site of the Banff National Park Administration Building), piping mineral water to the site from the Upper Hot Springs.

That same year Brett also constructed the "Grand View Villa" near the site of the Upper Hot Springs. At first all that Brett provided at the site was a

The Honourable
Robert G. Brett

1.3-by-2 m (4-by-6 ft.) pit dug into the ground and supplied with warm water from the springs. Business was so good that by the fall of 1886 Brett had constructed The Grand View Villa — a magnificent three-storey structure overlooking the Bow Valley near the site of the present-day Rimrock Hotel. It could accommodate 50 guests and 40 patients.

Brett was also quick to exploit the properties of the "curative" properties of the mineral water with another daring enterprise. In 1910 Brett began Banff's first souvenir business when he established the Banff Bottling Works, selling the mineral water under the label "Banff Lithia Water."

35

# If We Can't Export the Scenery

With the arrival of the railway, Banff was ready for a new age of discovery and began to flourish. As there were no roads leading into the park, Banff was only accessible by rail and the CPR did its utmost to keep it that way. In this era of "exclusiveness," Banff became the domain of the rich and famous. The construction of the Banff Springs Hotel in 1888 only enhanced this image.

How much influence did the CPR have in the development of Banff as a resort? After all, wasn't the government deeply indebted to the railroad for keeping British Columbia in Confederation and wasn't the CPR ultimately responsible for creation of the Hot Springs Reserve? The Vice-President of the CPR, William Cornelius Van Horne, certainly thought so and began to promote the Rockies as a major tourist and revenue-producing region for the railroad. Van Horne's philosophy was simple: "If we can't export the scenery, we'll import the tourists."

William Cornelius
Van Horne

# The Banff Springs Hotel

The Banff Springs
Hotel

As grand and prosperous as Dr. Brett's endeavours were, they would pale in the face of the plans William Cornelius Van Horne had for Banff. Van Horne was the former superintendent of the Chicago, Milwaukee, and St. Paul Railroad before coming to Canada in 1882 as the general manager of the CPR. Within two years, Van Horne had become vice-president of the CPR and intent on making Banff the prime tourist attraction in Canada; with huge monetary benefits to the railway of course!

Van Horne's plan was to establish a system of luxurious hotels through the Rockies along the CPR's main line to capitalize not only on the drawing power of the hot springs but also on the scenery of the Rocky Mountains. Van Horne began constructing what he would later call the "Finest Hotel on the North American Continent" on a promontory commanding a spectacular view of the Bow River Valley and the Fairholme Range. Construction of the hotel began in the winter of 1886 and opened to its first patrons in 1888. Its 250 rooms were the epitome of luxury, catering to every of the discriminating traveller at a cost of $3.50 and upwards per day.

# Bow Falls

Mt. Brewtster

Bow Falls

Very early on the morning of August 17, 1858, James Hector instructed his party to begin their journey up the Bow Valley following the trail they had cleared the previous day. He related that, meanwhile, he and Nimrod:

*... set off to see a fine fall on the river, which lay about three miles out of the direct course. A high hill (Tunnel Mtn.) stands out in the centre of the valley, and it is in breaking past this that the river is compressed into a very narrow spout-like channel, and then leaps over a ledge of rocks about 40 feet in height. Above the rocky contractions of the channel the river is dilated and sluggish, and the valley is filled up with large swampy lakes ...*

James Hector became the first tourist to view Bow Falls, one of Banff's most popular natural attractions.

## Almost a Hydro Plant

As the population of Banff and the number of tourists increased each year, so too did the need for public services; water, sewage and electrical facilities had to be expanded. In the 1903 annual report of the Department of the Interior Superintendent Howard Douglas thought that Banff's beauty spot, Bow Falls, could solve one of the areas municipal needs: "The Bow Falls afford unlimited water power for electrical lighting and water power, and although no estimate has been furnished as to the probable cost of installing a plant, it would seem from an examination of the locality that the cost of installation would not be very heavy." Fortunately, this suggestion by Douglas did not come to fruition and future generations of tourists will continue to marvel at the beauty of the falls.

# The Vermilion Lakes

A consequence of the last period of glaciation was the formation of a huge post-glacial lake in the Valley of the Bow west of Banff. This prehistoric lake, called Glacial Lake Vermilion, was much larger and perhaps 5 m deeper than it is today. Glacial moraines that dammed and then altered the flow pattern of the ancestral Bow River produced it. As the new channel for the Bow River cut through and eroded the rock between Tunnel and Rundle Mtns., it was like pulling the plug in a gigantic bathtub. Eventually water levels subsided and the

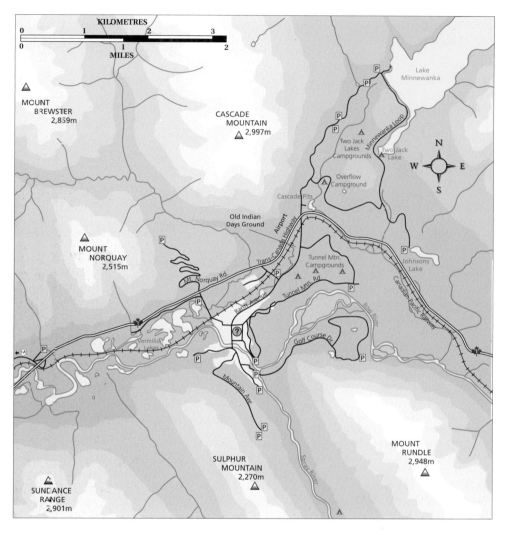

**Town of Banff and surrounding area**

three Vermilion Lakes we see today were formed and the wetlands associated with them gradually evolved.

Each year millions of people whiz along the Trans-Canada Highway, above what Hector called the valley with the "large swampy lakes," and below the south-facing slopes of Mt. Norquay, without ever realizing that people had been stopping there for the past 11,000 years! When archaeologists began digging here in the mid-1980s, prior to the twinning of the highway, they were surprised to find evidence of human habitation dating back to the end of the last

period of glaciation.

We know of their passing because of the clues they left: stone tools, tool fragments, burned fire hearths, bone fragments of the animals they hunted, and in some cases even parts of their primitive dwellings. To date, archaeologists have found at least eight campsites older than 9,500 years, neatly preserved in layers. On the floor of one of the oldest campsites archaeologists unearthed a pair of post holes that followed an arc of stone debris surrounding a hearth and an outline of what might be Canada's oldest house! The site was carbon dated to almost 11,000 years ago, near the end of the last glaciation.

These sites were not chosen randomly, but seem to have been chosen because they provided access to abundant game, clean water, wood for fuel, stone for tools, and the warmth of a south-facing slope. Ancient peoples were occupying campsites on the shores of the Vermilion Lakes thousands of years before the Egyptians began building the great pyramids!

# Peaks around Town

## Cascade Mtn. 2998 m

This is the mountain everyone first sets eyes on when entering Banff National Park and it is the most photographed mountain from Banff townsite. It is also a historically significant mountain because of the prominent position it occupies in the Bow Valley. The first recorded ascent of the mountain occurred in 1887 when L.B. Stewart and T.E. Wilson tramped up today's most popular scramblers' route, the long non-technical southwest ridge. This "non-technical" route is not to be taken lightly and in recent years has been the scene of four fatal accidents.

### Mini-ha-pa

Water has been cascading down the face of this mountain since time immemorial and it is probably the first landmark most tourists notice travelling west on the Trans-Canada Highway. Generations of Kootenay and Stoneys used it as a landmark to guide them through this valley. Early in the morning of August 15, 1858, Hector's guide Nimrod used this same waterfall to guide his party to this site where they camped. Hector's description is much as it is today, as they finally reached "a beautiful little prairie at the base of the 'Mountain where the water falls' [Mini-ha-pa] as the Indian name has it, or the Cascade Mountain."

Every early explorer to the Rock-

ies has commented on this landmark. Sir George Simpson passed it in 1841, but was clearly not impressed with the waterfall, and simply noted "a stream of water which, though of very considerable volume, looked like a thread of silver on the grey rock." He was too busy racing around the world to be enamoured by the cascade. That was not the case when Father Pierre-Jean de Smet viewed the cascade in 1845. He described a mountain from which a "beautiful crystalline fountain issues from the centre of a perpendicular

Top: Cascade Mtn.

Bottom: *Mini-ha-pa*

Mt. Norquay

Mt. Brewster

Sir John Norquay

Top: Mt. Norquay, without its scars, from near the junction of the Bow Valley Parkway and the Trans-Canada Highway

Bottom: Mt. Brewster from trail to Cascade Amphitheatre

rock about five hundred feet high, and then pours its water over the plain in foam and mist."

## Mt. Norquay 2522 m

The mountain that supports some of Canada's finest and most difficult ski runs was named in honour of Sir John Norquay (1841–89), who served in the Legislature and later became Premier of Manitoba (1878–89). John Norquay was a proud man of Métis heritage who was orphaned as a young boy. Brought up and educated by many caring families, Norquay became fluent in six languages, an ability that would later benefit him as premier of his province.

Norquay was an outstanding orator and an equally impressive figure, standing over six feet tall and weighing around three hundred pounds. His leadership qualities became evident during the Riel Rebellion. Louis Riel may have been spokesperson for the Métis, but

Norquay was their leader. His ability to support Riel's aims, while opposing his tactics, was instrumental in winning provincial status for Manitoba in 1870. Proud of his Métis ancestry, Norquay always acted with the highest personal integrity and was intensely loyal to his people.

Local legend credits Norquay with first ascent of the mountain named in his honour, but that is simply not true. What is true is that one year prior to his death in 1889, when his health was seriously failing, Norquay scrambled partway up the peak but did not reach the summit. That honour would later fall to N.W. Greenham in 1917.

## Mt. Brewster 2859 m

Mt. Brewster is the southern most peak of a ridge that extends north for approximately 19 km. From Banff, Mt. Brewster appears framed in the "V" between Mt. Norquay and Cascade Mtn. In 1934 the peak was named to commemorate the Brewster family, perhaps the most famous pioneer family in the annals of Banff National Park. Many landmarks, including a creek, a glacier, and a rock, were also named in

their honour, but particularly for John, and his son Jim (1832–1947), a pioneer outfitter and guide and the best known of John's four sons.

John, patriarch of the Brewster family hailed from Kingston, Ontario. After spending a few years in Winnipeg, he joined his brother William who was a carpenter working on the construction of the bathhouse at the Cave and Basin in 1886. William had also set up a dairy farm west of Vermil on Lakes to supply the town with fresh milk. John's four sons and wife Bella were brought to Banff on St. Patrick's Day, 1888.

Bill and Jim, the two eldest Brewster sons, were befriended by William Twin, a Stoney who educated the two boys in the ways of the wilderness and mountain travel. Quickly, Jim became a proficient guide and was once employed by the esteemed Charles E. Fay for a traverse of Abbot Pass to Lake O'Hara in 1897. Fay commented that the young Jim "would make a capital guide with proper training. A little too fresh just now and fond of telling big stories." Advertising themselves as "W & J Brewster, Guides and Packers," the two boys formally entered the outfitting business and entered the big time when the CPR asked

them to represent the company at the Sportsmen's Show at Madison Square Gardens in 1902. By 1905 they held exclusive rights to the livery and outfitting concession at the CPR's Banff Springs Hotel.

With the advent of the automobile and the construction of major roads into and around Banff, the CPR gradually lost its hold as the major form of transportation into Banff National Park. Tourism was changing forever from the pastime of the "rich and famous" to people from all walks of life — people who simply wanted to enjoy and experience the grandeur of the Rocky Mountains. The Brewster family was quick to recognize this change and by 1905 was contracted by the CPR to service the guests at the Banff Springs Hotel. Little did anyone realize at the time that the birth of a prosperous tour group was about to begin.

## Mt. Rundle 2949 m

Cascade Mtn. may dominate the skyline around Banff, but Mt. Rundle is surely the most famous peak in the vicinity. Mt. Rundle is a classic example of a dip slope mountain with its flat, tabletop side evident from Banff and its sheer eastern

Left: William Twin and his brother Joshua

Right: Jim Brewster

Mt. Rundle

Goat Range

**The town of Banff from road to Mt. Norquay**

cliffs providing the backdrop along the Trans-Canada Highway. This 15 km long massif has seven distinct peaks. It was named by James Hector in honour of Reverend Robert Terrill Rundle (1811–96), a Methodist missionary who devoted the greater part of his life administering to the Cree, Stoneys, and Blackfoot of the region.

Who was this legendary Methodist missionary? Robert Terrill Rundle was born in the county of Cornwall, England on June 11, 1811, the son of Robert Rundle (1778–1851) and Grace Carvosso (1781–1838). Born into a religious Methodist family replete with preachers and missionaries, the young Robert was influenced by their teachings and was ordained by the Wesleyan Missionary Society on March 8, 1840.

In 1840 the Hudson's Bay Company advertised for a "young man to go out as a missionary to the Indians in the far west and to act as a Company chaplain in the same district." Rundle answered that call and began his journey to the New World on March 16, 1840, arriving at Fort Edmonton in October. For the next eight years his was a mission of love as he ministered to the needs of his native brethren. Not only did he preach Christianity to the Stoneys and the Cree, but he also became totally immersed in their way of life, language, and customs.

Rundle suffered many hardships and had many accidents during his eight-year stay before ill health finally forced him to leave the country he so dearly loved in 1848. Six years later he died in Scotland. Perhaps the greatest tribute to Rundle came from his beloved native congregation: "Poor he came among us, and poor he went away, leaving us rich."

**Reverend Robert Terrill Rundle**

## The Legend of the First Ascent

The journals of Reverend Rundle provide the first detailed account of an attempted ascent of a mountain in the Bow Valley, somewhere near Canmore or the Lake Minnewanka region. A remarkable tale has grown around this attempt and has somehow worked its way to the slopes of Mt. Rundle itself. This tantalizing account describes the feeling every climber has experienced at one time or another, including fear, hunger, thirst, fatigue, over-extension, and finally anxiety brought on by being lost. Regardless of the mountain in question, the following narrative, in Rundle's own words from his diary entry for Saturday, November 19, 1844, has become part of the lore of the Canadian Rockies

*Am now climbing a mountain. Here are neo veins, perhaps a spar, in the bed of rock where I am now sitting. I became quite ill thro' fatigue &c but was in good spirits when climbing, until I was very high up. I made two attempts to get up an elevation but could not succeed. Rocks very steep — felt very weak, so weak, that at last I was near fainting whilst passing over a projecting ledge or rock. What a moment of anxiety. I have some recollection of calling to the Almighty to assist me & praised be His name, my prayer was heard. I descended to the next stage. It was presumptuous of me I know but I began again to see if I could not find a better way to scale higher but I could not succeed so I now abandoned my design & commenced descending. I was not careful about the road & had great difficulty in descending. I was very weak from want of food, having left without breakfast, & began to feel afraid ever & anon too I heard the moving stones, which terrified me. How hard, too, to pass along the steep sloping sides sloping away to fearful descent. At length, however, I reached the bottom, but how was I to get to the encampment? I had lost the road. Very tired, weak, & unwell. Heard gun fired!! & so guided!! Reached at last, thanks to Providence. Took some medicine & had breakfast at sunset.*

For the record, legendary surveyor, J.J. McArthur, completed the first ascent of the highest peak of Mt. Rundle in 1888. This peak is another of the most popular scrambles in the Banff region that is not to be taken lightly. In the recent past, misjudgment has led to serious errors, resulting in five fatal accidents.

## Sulphur Mtn. 2451 m

Sulphur Mtn is part of a long ridge that overhangs the valley of the Spray River. James Hector originally referred to this peak as "Terrace Mountain," but that was changed in favour of its present name in reference to the ever-present smell of sulphur emanating from the hot springs that boil up from deep within the bowels of the mountain. The summit can be reached via a popular 5.5 km hiking trail, but is most often reached by the even more popular gondola.

The gondola was the brainchild of John Jaeggi, a native of Switzerland who came to Banff in 1924. After a near fatal accident trying to manoeuver a modified farm tractor on the switchbacks of the trail leading to the summit, Jaeggi hit on the idea of constructing a gondola to the top of the peak. For a number of

Hans "John" Jaeggi
ca. 1920s

Left: Norman Bethune Sanson

Right:
The meteorological observatory as it appeared in 1909

years he tried to obtain financial backing for his project in Canada, but each proposal was turned down. Finally, Jaeggi found investors in his native Switzerland and construction of the gondola began in 1958. The gondola was opened to tourists the following year and today Jaeggi's project quickly and efficiently transports more than 500,000 visitors to the top of the mountain every year.

## Sanson Pk. 2270 m

The highest point at the north end of Sulphur Mtn. has been christened Sanson Pk. in honour of one of Banff's legendary residents, Norman Bethune Sanson (1862–1949). Sanson was a jack of all trades — accountant, meteorologist, naturalist, hiker, scrambler, and curator of the Banff Park Museum from 1896 to1931. Born in Toronto to a distinguished family of professionals, young Sanson joined the Queen's Own Rifles and took part in the Riel Rebellion of 1885 before coming to Banff in 1892 where he finally found his niche.

His first job was as an accountant at Dr. Brett's Sanatorium Hotel, but he soon took on the work of helping local meteorologist George Paris collect weather data from the summit of Sulphur Mtn. Sanson chose the site for the weather observatory on the north summit of Sulphur Mtn., which was built in 1903 and restored to its original stature in 1992. From then until 1931 Sanson climbed the mountain every week, and then bi-weekly until his retirement. On the occasion of his 1000th ascent his friends arranged for a sunrise breakfast atop the peak, catered by the staff of the Banff Springs Hotel.

When George MacLeod, the first curator of the Banff Museum, died in 1896, he was replaced by Sanson even though Sanson was not technically qualified for the job. This mattered little as Sanson's enthusiasm soon overcame his lack of technical training and he became the driving force behind the museum for the next 36 years.

Norman Bethune Sanson loved the mountains and hiking was what he enjoyed most. It has been estimated that Sanson hiked more than 32,000 km in his beloved Rocky Mountains. One year before his death in May 1949, the summit with the meteorological observatory was christened Sanson Pk. in his honour. Sanson chose his own epitaph for his tombstone, reading simply, "Gone Higher."

# Sundance Range
# 2900 m

The Sundance Range consists of a spectacular ridge, stretching for approximately 24 km from just east of Allenby Pass north to the Bow River. The highest point of this ridge is 2900 m, but it consists of many minor peaks over 2700 m in altitude. Legend has it that the Stoneys practised the religious ritual known as the Sun Dance near this range. In the 19th century this ceremony, held but once a year, was the most spectacular and important religious ceremony of the Plains Natives. It was usually held around the time of the summer solstice and lasted from four to eight days. The rite celebrated a renewal, the spiritual rebirth of the participants and their relatives, as well as the regeneration of the living earth with all of its components.

During the dance participants usually went through self-inflicted torture by having pieces of bone or wood skewered into their skin and tied to the sun-pole They would then dance around the pole tugging until the skin broke free. The gift of one's own body was seen as the highest form of sacrifice and the torture came to symbolize rebirth. Thus, the dancer was reborn, mentally, physically, and spiritually, along with the buffalo and the entire universe.

Top: The Sundance Range

Bottom: A Stoney Sun Dance Lodge, Morley, Alberta, 1926

# Devil's Gap Route

## Lake Minnewanka: "Lake of the Water Spirit"

This remarkable photo reveals the "Ghost Lakes" and the eastern end of Lake Minnewanka prior to flooding of the valley in 1910

On August 15, 1858, Hector had reached the base of *Mini-ha-pa*, Cascade Mtn., where he camped for the night. That evening he was visited by a Stoney he had met before leaving Old Bow Fort. The Stoney told Hector:

*[That he had] come through the first range by a pass to the south of "devil's Head," in which he says there is a lake the length of half a day's march, where they catch the finest trout and white fish in the country. At the upper end of the lake, which sends a stream into Bow River just below where we camped, he says there is a "height of land" to be crossed,*
*and from the other side of which rises Deadman's River.*

This Stoney was describing to Hector the ancient route through Devil's Gap, Lake Minnewanka, as well as the location of present-day Ghost River. Hector was also informed that this same Stoney had once guided Reverend Rundle by that route to this same camping place beneath the "Mountain where the water falls."

The entire region surrounding Lake Minnewanka is steeped in superstition. *Minnee-wah-kah*, the Stoney term for the lake, has many translations, including "Lake of the Water Spirit" and "Water of the Spirits." The lake has also been called

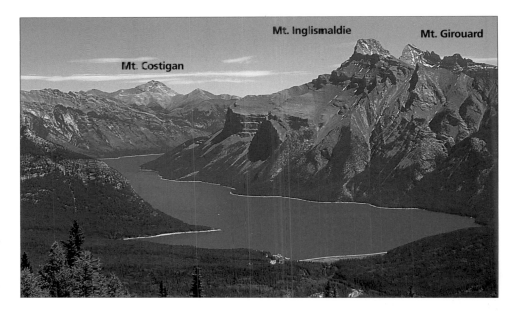

Mt. Costigan     Mt. Inglismaldie     Mt. Girouard

"Wendigo Lake," "Devil's Lake," "Dead Lake," "Ghost Lake," and sometimes "The Lake of the Evil Water-Spirit." All of these names had their origins in superstition or events related to evil spirits. One such event is the basis of the name "Wendigo," or Cannibal Lake. According to this legend, the lake was inhabited by a cannibalistic creature that was half-man, half-fish. This creature preyed on unsuspecting people and was greatly annoyed by noise. One day a group of Stoney women with children were fishing on the lake and began to sing. This annoyed the creature, which reached out and grabbed one of the occupants. Her companions began to slash at the creatures arm in an attempt to free their companion but this caused the boat to capsize. Only one of the fishing party lived to tell the story and since that time, no Stoney dares to venture onto the lake.

Even the Ghost River to the east was considered to be haunted and the source of many tales. Stories abound of ghosts visiting the graves of slain warriors in search of skulls or of the wailing throughout the night of those slain in battle.

Perhaps the most famous legend of Ghost River, recounted by Hugh Dempsey in *Indians of the Rocky Mountain Parks*, tells the story of a stampeding buffalo herd, which disturbed a Stoney camp each night but was never seen by the people:

*One evening a hunter promised to find the source of the strange sounds. He saddled his horse and tied it next to his lodge. As soon as he heard the sounds of hoofbeats, he jumped on his horse and pursued the herd. Ahead he saw the buffalo and a man riding a grey horse. He spurred his own horse forward, trying to get a glimpse of the stranger's face, but as soon as he caught up with him, the man and the buffalo disappeared. Ever since that incident, the nearby stream has been called Ghost River.*

In 1841 Sir George Simpson referred to the Lake as "Peechee" after his Métis guide Alex Piché. Six years later Rundle referred to it as "Wild Cat" or "Lynx Lake," the Stoney translation of the name Piché.

**Lake Minnewanka as it appears today**

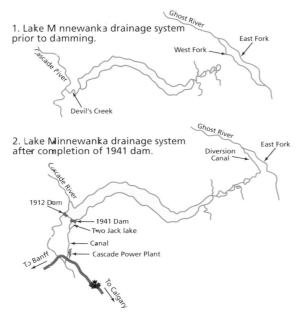

1. Lake Minnewanka drainage system prior to damming.

Ghost River
East Fork
West Fork
Cascade River
Devil's Creek

2. Lake Minnewanka drainage system after completion of 1941 dam.

Ghost River
East Fork
Diversion Canal
Cascade River
1912 Dam
1941 Dam
Two Jack lake
Canal
Cascade Power Plant
To Banff
To Calgary

The drainage pattern of Lake Minnewanka before and after damming the lake

George Mercer Dawson officially named the lake "Devil's Lake" but George Stewart, the first Park Superintendent, thought the name too ominous and renamed it Lake Minnewanka in 1888. Stewart thought that this name, a corruption of the Stoney translation for "Lake of the Water Spirit," would be less threatening and more favourable to tourism.

## Prehistoric Humans at the Lake

Between 1997 and 1999 archaeologists from the University of Calgary uncovered evidence of human occupation on the shores of Lake Minnewanka dating back over 10,000 years. Most of the site is under water due to the damming of the lake, but sections of it become exposed in early spring when the water level drops. Artifacts from an excavation on the north shore of the lake include three fireplaces, a bison horn, and the bones of an extinct species of mountain sheep. In addition, two styles of spear points have been unearthed — a Plainview Point (over

11,000 years old) and an Agate Basin Point (around 10,000 years old), both of which were found next to ancient firepits. Three such firepits have been excavated at this site. Radioactive carbon dating of artifacts from other levels could be even older, establishing this site as the oldest known archaeological site in the Province of Alberta.

Archaeologists suggest that Lake Minnewanka was probably an ideal site for these ancient peoples. There was plenty of water and mineral licks to attract an assortment of game, the lake supported a huge fish population, and nearby Banff chert offered a supply of stone for making tools. In addition, the south-facing site provided warmth from the sun for these early humans who lived at the end of the last ice age.

## Damming the Lake Changes the Landscape

How different the valley and lake are today compared to just over 100 years ago. An insatiable need for electrical power was about to change the structure of the valley that had existed in its pristine state since the last glaciation. By 1895, a small resort community known as Minnewanka Landing had been constructed on the shores of the lake. To protect the community wharf from flooding, a small log dam was constructed on Devil's Creek. It did little to alter the shoreline but was an omen of things to come. The lake, at this time, was still linked by a narrow channel to three adjoining lakes farther east.

In 1910 the federal Government granted Calgary Power permission to construct a storage dam on the west shore of Lake Minnewanka. This caused water levels in the lake to rise about 6 m and it inundated an area of approximately 1000 acres. A penstock, turbine, surge tower, and generating plant downstream of the Cascade River were also included in the plans to supply electrical power to the growing community of Banff. The Cascade generating station began supplying power to Banff in 1924. More was yet to come.

The need for electrical power for Banff, Canmore, and Calgary continued to grow as these communities increased in size. The Dominion Parks Branch did everything possible to resist Calgary Power's application to develop additional water-storage capacity at Lake Minnewanka in compliance with the conservationist policies developed for national parks.

In 1940 Calgary Power again applied for permission to enhance the storage capacity of Lake Minnewanka to supply electricity to the new explosive plant in Calgary. The new dam was constructed and the Cascade power plant was completed in 1941. This time the dam completely changed the landscape forever. Floodwaters backed up into the upper drainage of the Cascade River, submerged the 1912 dam, and nearly doubled the size of the lake. This raised the level of the lake by approximately 25 m and lengthened

Devil's Canyon Dam

it to 28 km.

Construction of the power plant also changed the drainage pattern of the Cascade River, Ghost River, and Lake Minnewanka drainage systems forever. To create and sustain this huge body of water, a canal was constructed to divert water from the west fork of the Ghost River into the east end of the lake and the Cascade River was diverted from its natural course. Water from Lake Minnewanka is channelled into a system of canals, into flumes, over cliffs, and into the turbines of the Cascade power station.

# Devil's Gap

Most people are surprised to learn that the preferred route in to the Rocky Mountains was through the gap between Orient Point (2656 m) and Mt. Costigan (2980 m), which became known as Devil's Gap. This route provided easy access from the Ghost River to Lake Minnewanka and then to the Bow River near the base of Cascade Mtn. The route was safe and the distinctive shapes of Orient Point and Devil's Head, which were visible on the horizon for many kilometres, acted as landmarks.

## Devil's Head 2796 m

In 1841, when James Sinclair led a group of settlers bound for the Oregon Territory through this region, anxiety and an air of trepidation seized the party. They were well aware of the superstitious beliefs associated with Devil's Head. Geneva

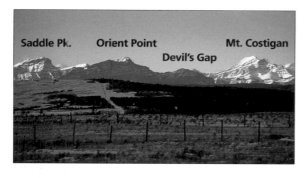

Saddle Pk.    Orient Point      Mt. Costigan

Devil's Gap

*The "gates" guarding the entrance to Devil's Gap*

Lent wrote, "As the train drew closer to the main range of the Rockies, a great grey escarpment seemed to loom directly before them, as if to block all entry to the mountains. The Cree Indians so feared this peak they made propitiatory offerings to its Manitou in the form of pipes, tobacco, and decorated tomahawks on certain of its ledges."

Although Devil's Head is not now located within Banff National Park, in 1902 it was once part of the expanded Rocky Mountains National Park. Devil's Head acted as a beacon that led parties to the gap into the Front Ranges of the Rocky Mountains. So distinctive is the shape of this mountain that Peter Fidler referred to it by name in his journal in 1792 and Anthony Henday must have seen it in 1754 although he makes no mention of it. Even today, owing to its unique shape, it is one of the most recognizable mountains that can be seen from Calgary.

What is the origin of this ominous name? No one is completely sure, but generations of aboriginals were known to both fear and revere the peak. The native peoples thought that it was the home of evil spirits and the Cree feared this mountain so much they often left offerings on its slopes to appease these spirits. When the "Little Emperor," Governor George Simpson passed this way in 1841 he suggested that the shape of the mountain resembled some dreadful face.

# The First Tourists to Banff

*Sir George Simpson*

Given the circumstances previously discussed, it is not surprising that, in 1841, Cree and Stoney guides led the first Europeans into the Rockies via Devil's Gap. They would become the first tourists to visit Banff National Park.

## The First Dignitary: Sir George Simpson

Shortly after being knighted by Queen Victoria in March 1841, Sir George Simpson (governor of the Hudson's Bay Company), embarked on his journey around the world. His goal was to set the record for the fastest circumnavigation of the globe. Simpson had originally intended to take the more northerly route over Athabasca Pass, but was advised to avoid that route because it was in flood. Simpson's Métis guide, Alexis Piché, then suggested to the governor that a faster, more southerly route existed through Devil's Gap.

The Simpson party arrived at the north shore of this beautiful lake in the first week of August 1841 where Simpson recorded this in his journal:

*In the morning we entered a defile between mountain ridges, marching for nine hours* through dense woods. This valley, which was from two to three miles in width contained four beautiful lakes, communicating with each other by small streams; and the fourth of the series, which was about fifteen miles by three, we named after Peechee as being our guide's usual home.

Simpson was of course referring to present-day Lake Minnewanka, which he wanted to name Peechee, after his Métis guide. He apparently had trouble pronouncing the Métis name and corrupted it to Peechee! Simpson did not linger at the lake and quickly continued up the Bow Valley and across the Great Divide.

# The First Settler: James Sinclair

On June 3, 1841, James Sinclair began a journey from Fort Gary intent on leading a group of 100 settlers across the Rockies to settle in the then disputed Oregon Territory. At Fort Edmonton, Sinclair hired the great Chief of the Wetaskiwin Cree named Maskipitoon, also known as *Ech-tow-wees-ka-zeet* ("He Who Has Eyes Behind Him") or "Broken Arm" (due to a childhood deformity) to guide the party across the mountains. Maskipitoon was miffed that Simpson had not chosen him to guide the governor's party and assured Sinclair that he knew of a new and quicker route through the mountains that no white person had ever travelled. Sinclair, never enamoured by Simpson's character, jumped at the opportunity to beat Simpson to the Pacific Ocean.

The Sinclair party passed Devil's Head and entered the valley containing Lake Minnewanka. However, instead of following the traditional route along the north shore of the lake, Maskipitoon followed an ancient trail on the south shore and

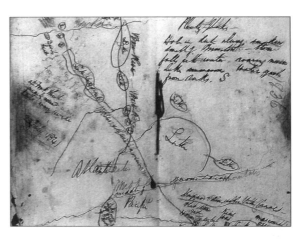

then down Carrot Creek to the Bow Valley in the vicinity of present-day Canmore. They then entered the Spray River Valley, passing through the southern reaches of future Banff National Park across White Man Pass. Although this was but a brief encounter, Sinclair became the second "tourist" to pass through the future national park.

# The First Missionary: Robert Terrill Rundle

The third visitor to enter the valley was the Wesleyan missionary Reverend Robert Terrill Rundle. Rundle became interested in this region early in 1847 after Peechee drew a sketch map for him showing lakes, rivers, and passes along the route of the Simpson party. This sketch became the earliest detailed map ever known to have been made of part of the future national park.

On February 7, 1847, he spent a weekend at Lake Minnewanka. Rundle described it as "the most interesting lake I ever saw." He recorded that the lake was "several miles in length, embedded in the mountain which rise in grandeur." On the morning of his departure he blazed a tree with the inscription "RTR July 1, 1847" and left his beloved mountains forever. The damming of the lake has unfortunately doomed this

**Map of Lake Minnewanka sketched in Rundle's journal in 1847**

51

Henry Warre's watercolour, *Rocky Mountains near the Bow River, July 23, 1845*

historic anecdote to history under many metres of water.

## The First Artist: Captain Henry Warre

In the middle of the 19th century, tensions between Great Britain and the United States were growing over the disputed Oregon Territory. The British government organized a secret military mission to determine the best way to transport military equipment and supplies across the mountain barrier. Captain Henry Warre and Lieutenant Mervin Vavasour were asked to lead this clandestine reconnaissance.

They were to appear in the guise of gentlemen of leisure on a sport hunting expedition and, as such, briefly visited the Bow Valley in the region of Banff in July 1845. The two "spies" followed the same route as that of James Simpson in 1841, but after losing most of their horses and suffering much hardship their final report did not speak favourably of a usable route across the Rockies.

*Without attempting to describe the numerous Defiles through which we passed, or the difficulty of forcing a passage through the burnt Forests, and over the high land, we may venture to assert, that Sir George Simpson's idea of transporting troops ... with their stores, etc. through such an extent of uncultivated Country and over such impracticable Mountains would appear to Us quite unfeasible.*

However, their adventure was historically significant for an entirely different reason; Warre was an accomplished artist and became the first person to sketch and paint the splendour of the Rocky Mountains. He published his works in a book entitled *Sketches in North America and the Oregon Territory* in 1848. One watercolour, *Rocky Mountains near the Bow River, July 23, 1845,* (shown above) clearly depicts two of the most famous mountains in Banff National Park, the cliffs of Mt. Rundle and Cascade Mtn. Produced from a sketch near present-day Canmore, the watercolour became the first landscape of mountains in the park. Legions of artists would later flock to the Rockies to capture this scenery on canvas.

## The First Jesuit: Father Pierre-Jean de Smet

Father de Smet was a Jesuit Missionary who worked among the Kootenay in the Oregon Territory before he was convinced to extend his missionary work eastward across the Rockies into Blackfoot territory. In 1845 Father de Smet used the same pass as that of Sinclair to cross the Rockies and became a diligent observer

Father de Smet

of important landmarks. He too left evidence of his crossing of the Great Divide, by erecting the "Cross of Peace" near the summit of White Man Pass. Father de Smet wrote, "The Christian's standard, the cross has been reared at the sources of these two rivers [White Man Pass]: may it be a sign of salvation and peace to all the scattered and itinerant tribes east and west of these gigantic and lurid mountains." George Dawson allegedly found remnants of this cross years later while working for the Boundary Commission.

Below top: Lake Minnewanka separates peaks of the Palliser Range (left) from the Fairholme Range (right)

Bottom: Mt. Aylmer is just visible peeking over the shoulder of Mt. Astley (middle)

# Peaks Surrounding the Lake

Two mountain ranges surround Lake Minnewanka. Peaks belonging to the Palliser Range form the backdrop on the north shore of the lake, while mountains of the Fairholme Range border the south shore and are the first peaks to be seen when approaching the Rockies from Calgary. Reverend Terrill Rundle made the first recorded observations of the geography of the Lake Minnewanka region on July 1, 1847 when he wrote, "Behind the encampment two mountains strata, horizontal. In the valley, each side either oblique, sloping from E [east] to west, downwards or horizontal, but the greater part hori [horizontal] Scarcely any vertical. Reached Dead River [Ghost River] ... It runs under and some distance it comes again to the surface near the forks of the River."

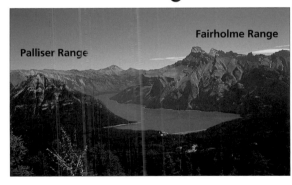

Palliser Range

Fairholme Range

Mt. Astley

Mt. Aylmer

# The Palliser Range

J.J. McArthur (above) and his assistant W.S. Drewry (bottom) demonstrate their climbing skills

(1842–1923), who became the Inspector-General of the Canadian Militia and later served as the president of the Kootenay Gold Mines. A second possibility is that it was named after his younger brother Frederick Whitworth (1850–1920), an engineer for the CPR and surveyor of the upper Columbia Valley.

However, the most likely scenario is that J.J. McArthur named the peak in honour of his birthplace, Aylmer, Quebec, after he completed the first ascent of the mountain in 1889. By coincidence, Aylmer, Quebec was named for McArthur's grandfather (1775–1850) who was the Governor General of Canada from 1831–1835.

## Mt. Astley 2869 m

This unofficial name applies to the peak separated from Mt. Aylmer by Aylmer Pass. It was named in honour of Charles D. Astley, who lived at the mountain's foot for 20 years. With his brother Willoughby, he operated the CPR boat concession at Lake Minnewanka in the late 1800s. Norman Sanson claims to have come across a report of the Geological Survey Branch of the Department of Mines, dated 1910, that attached Astley's name to the peak, but to this day the name remains unofficial. Willoughby Astley later moved to Lake Louise where he managed the CPR Chalet.

The Palliser Range was named after Captain John Palliser, the leader of the three-year Palliser Expedition that explored much of the southern Rockies of western Canada. Mt. Aylmer is the highest peak in the range and indeed the highest peak in the Eastern Slopes of the Front Ranges.

## Mt. Aylmer 3163 m

Both Sir George Simpson and James Sinclair must have seen this impressive pyramidal-shaped mountain when they passed through the region in 1841, but they make no mention of it. There is considerable confusion regarding the origin of the name of this mountain and there are three possible scenarios. First, the mountain was named after Mathew the eighth Baron of Aylmer

## Mt. Costigan 2978 m

Mt. Costigan was named after the Honourable John Costigan, a prominent member of the New Brunswick legislature who later became a senator. Together with Orient Point (2636 m), these two peaks mark the easternmost boundary of Banff National Park and form part of the "gateway" to the historic passage through the Front Ranges called Devil's Gap.

54

# The Fairholme Range

Mt. Costigan

Mt. Inglismaldie

Mt. Aylmer

Devil's Head

Blue Rock Mtn.

The small group of peaks of the Fairholme Range that lies within Banff National Park is north of the Trans-Canada Highway and forms the eastern boundary of the park. They are the first peaks to be encountered when approaching the mountains from the east. Captain Palliser named the range in 1859 in honour of William Fairholme and his wife Grace, Palliser's oldest sister. It appears the entire family was adventurous — William's younger brother Walter lost his life on the ill-fated Franklin Expedition to the Arctic, and it was William's account of a hunting trip he made to Missouri in 1840 that fired the imagination of Palliser into proposing his famous expedition.

## Mt. Inglismaldie 3013 m

George Stewart, the first superintendent of Banff National Park, named this mountain after Inglismaldie Castle, in Scotland, the ancestral home of the Earl of Kintore. The castle was built in the late 16th century and acquired in 1635 by Sir John Carnegie, the Earl of Northesk. Why does a castle of no apparent historical significance warrant such an honour? The Earl of Kintore paid a visit to the Rockies in late 1887 and Park Superintendent Stewart felt obliged to recognize his visit by naming this peak after his ancestral castle. Park superintendents had a lot of power in the early years and would never get away with such indiscretion today.

**The Honourable John Costigan**

## Mt. Girouard 3010 m

Mt. Girouard was officially named in 1904 to honour Boer War hero Colonel Sir Edward Percy Girouard (1867–1932). He was the son of a judge of the Supreme Court of Canada and a graduate of the Royal Military College of Kingston, Ontario. He was commissioned into the British Army Royal Engineers in 1888

Panorama of peaks viewed from Highway 940

Sir Edward Percy Girouard

Top: Peaks of the Fairholme Range from the trail to Cascade Amphitheatre

Bottom: Peaks of the Fairholme Range viewed from Tunnel Mtn. Drive

where he rose to the rank of colonel in 1909.

At the age of 32, Girouard was made Director of Railways for the British forces in the Sudan (1899–1902) and was responsible for building a 588-mile railway across the Sudanese desert. Following the defeat of the Sudanese, he received the Distinguished Service Order. Girouard was reinstated in the British Army at the onset of the Boer War in 1899, and sent to South Africa as Director of Railways. For his actions during the war he was awarded a knighthood, the first Canadian ex-cadet to be so honoured.

In 1907 Sir Percy became High Commissioner to Northern Nigeria and became governor from 1908 to 1909. After the outbreak of World War I, Lord Kitchener summoned

Girouard back into the army with the rank of major general. Winston Churchill considered Girouard to be one of the most brilliant men of his times.

## Mt. Peechee 2935 m

George Mercer Dawson named this peak with a double summit in honour of Simpson's Métis guide Alexis Piché. Simpson so respected Piché for his character and knowledge of the mountains that, upon reaching Fort Colville, Oregon, Sir George presented his guide with his favourite telescope.

It is evident that Piché possessed unusual knowledge of routes across passes in the Rockies that were unknown to white people. Not only did he guide Simpson over an entirely new route to the Pacific, but in 1844 he drew a detailed sketch of the route for Reverend R.T. Rundle depicting the major landmarks. This sketch is the earliest known map detailing the region that would later become Banff National Park.

# A Tale of Two Guides

The two guides Alexis Piché and Maskipitoon played pivotal roles in the exploration of the Rocky Mountains and it is amazing how closely their two lives were intertwined. Alexis Piché guided Sir George Simpson; Maskipitoon led James Sinclair and may possibly have led Palliser across passes of the Great Divide never before seen by European explorers. Both Piché and Maskipitoon travelled with Reverend Rundle. Both were later murdered.

Piché had a love for gambling, a habit that would lead to his violent death. During a game of chance at Fort Edmonton on January 6, 1844 he staked and lost his horse to two brothers who had accompanied Father de Smet to

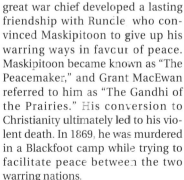

**Maskipitoon**

Rocky Mountain House. When Piché refused to deliver the animal they promptly shot him in the head and then murdered his son with a shot through the heart. The two murders occurred within a few steps of Reverend Rundle's tent and in a letter to Chief Factor Evans, Rundle wrote:

*And now alas! I am compelled to enter on a scene of blood! Will you believe it possible, my dear sir, when I tell you that two murders were committed at this place within a few seconds of time (literally a few seconds) and within a few steps of my tent? Alas! It is horribly true. What a shock to my feelings! Indeed it was some time before my poor nervous system would rally from it.*

Maskipitoon, a chief of the Wetaskiwin Cree, was a renowned and greatly feared warrior. He had collected more than his share of Blackfoot scalps and, in an apparent fit of rage, also collected the scalp of his wife over an alleged infidelity. His warlike nature ended when he was befriended by Reverend Rundle and converted to Christianity. This great war chief developed a lasting friendship with Rundle who convinced Maskipitoon to give up his warring ways in favour of peace. Maskipitoon became known as "The Peacemaker," and Grant MacEwan referred to him as "The Gandhi of the Prairies." His conversion to Christianity ultimately led to his violent death. In 1869, he was murdered in a Blackfoot camp while trying to facilitate peace between the two warring nations.

# The Ghost Towns

BANKHEAD ALTA.

Bankhead at the height of its mining operations, ca. 1920s

Since the entire region surrounding Lake Minnewanka is steeped in superstition, it is only fitting to end this chapter with a discussion of two ghost towns. In 1885 renowned geologist George Dawson reported vast reserves of high-rank coal in the Front Ranges. One of these reserves occurred in a gentle syncline that stretched between the slopes of Mt. Rundle and Cascade Mtn. from just north of Banff to south of Canmore. He named the deposit the Cascade Coal Basin. The coal was anthracite; hard, shiny jet-black, and it burned with intense heat and little smoke.

## Anthracite

In 1886 a small company named The Canadian Anthracite Company, based in Eau Claire, Wisconsin, opened a mine at Anthracite, 6.5 km (4 mi.) east of Banff, and in 1889 another mine near Canmore. In 1886 the coal-mining community of Anthracite began to flourish around these deposits. The town grew quickly to include a hotel, general store, restaurant, and of course a barber shop with adjacent pool hall. At its peak the town boasted a population of over 300 residents.

But alas, good times were not to last. The steeply slanted coal seams at Anthracite suffered from one major flaw; they were subject to flooding by the high water table of the Bow River Valley. Despite these problems, Anthracite continued to supply coal to the CPR main line until 1904 when it was abandoned in favour of a much larger operation at Bankhead.

## Bankhead

The canny William Cornelius Van Horne did not want to rely on coal from Canmore to supply his main line and so, by the summer of 1902, CPR geologists began mapping the deposits on the slopes of Cascade Mtn. There they discovered at least 12 major coal seams. The coal was termed semi-anthracite because it wasn't as hard as the classic type found at Anthracite but it was easy to mine.

In 1903 a company town named Bankhead was established and a town of considerable proportions began to grow at the base of Cascade Mountain, about 5 km east of Siding 29. At its peak, the town boasted a population of over 1000 residents and a residential area of around 100 homes. It also included a hotel, stores, several saloons, a restaurant, and its own school. The new town rivalled Banff in both size and activity.

The coal proved to be not of the high quality originally suspected, as it was too fine and easily broken. In order to overcome this problem, engineers decided to construct a briquette plant to convert the dust and fragments into a usable form. At its peak, Anthracite produced 1,000 tons of coal and 300 tons of briquettes a day, but the cost of producing these briquettes made the entire mining operation uneconomical.

The final blow to Bankhead came as a series of crippling strikes by the miners who protested dangerous conditions, exposure to toxic coal dust, and a pay scale so low that only barley allowed them to survive. On June 15, 1922, the Bankhead mine was closed forever.

Today all that remains of Bankhead are the ruins of the once teeming town and the original railroad station. Visitors can wander for hours through the ghost town, which is just off the roadway to Lake Minnewanka. The station can be viewed behind the Banff International Hostel just off Tunnel Mountain Road.

*The old Bankhead Station with a new coat of paint*

# The Bow Valley Parkway

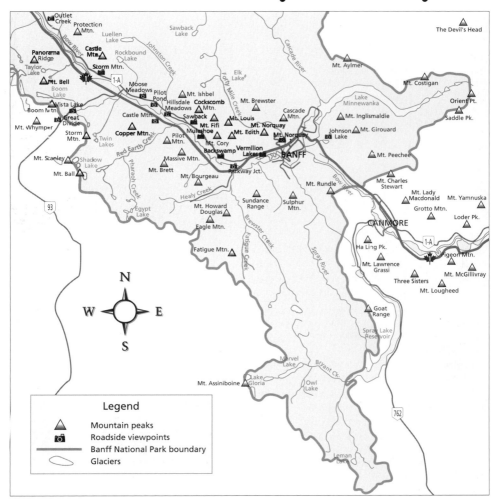

Legend

△ Mountain peaks
📷 Roadside viewpoints
— Banff National Park boundary
⌃ Glaciers

**Illustrated map of peaks and viewpoints in the Bow Valley in the Banff vicinity**

After visiting Bow Falls with Nimrod on the morning of August 17, 1858, James Hector continued his journey up the Bow Valley. He was in awe of its magnificence, and wrote:

*After a halt for two hours during the most intense heat, we again started and crossed over a low point of rocks, close to the river, where we entered the second great valley, which is of*

*magnificent proportions. All along the eastern side runs a wall of vertical beds, of light grey limestone, the serrated edges of which at once suggested the name of Sawback Range for them. The valley is three to four miles wide, and on the west side we have quite a change in the features of the mountains. The strata which compose them are nearly horizontal, and the mountains form cubical blocks or ranges of battlement-like precipices, while super-imposed masses resemble towers and bastions.*

Hector was entering the upper Bow Valley and accurately described the major characteristics that differentiate the Front Ranges from the Main Ranges. After nearly 100 million years the Sawback Range finally had a name.

Serrated peaks of the Sawback Range

# The Sawback Range

This range consists of a series of serrated peaks that run north from Mt. Edith along the Bow River to the mouth of Baker Creek. A number of high points along the range offer great climbing and a couple of the peaks have become world renowned. Mt. Isabel is the highest peak in the range but it is the spectacular vertical tower of Mt. Louis that attracts all the attention.

The stands of burnt forest, which appear on the slopes of the Sawback Range, were not ignited by lightning or carelessness. These slopes were set ablaze by Parks Canada during a prescribed burn in June 1993 in an effort re-establish a balance to the forest ecosystem brought about by nearly 75 years of fire prevention. Nearly 1000 ha were burnt.

## Mt. Louis 2862 m

Mt. Louis is the ultimate dogtooth mountain! Not only is it the most spectacular and famous peak of the Sawback Range, but also of the entire Front Ranges. One drawback is that it is as difficult to view as it is to ascend. Fortunately every visitor can catch a glimpse of this famous peak from the Cascade Power Plant when travelling west on the Trans-Canada Highway. The peak can also be viewed through the same "notch" on the Lake Minnewanka road as you approach Johnson's Lake.

This peak formed from vertically standing Devonian Limestone, was named in honour of Louis Beaufort Stewart (1861–1937), son of George Stewart, the first superintendent of then Rocky Mountains National Park. Louis Stewart was an accomplished land surveyor who accompanied Professor Norman J. Collie to the Rocky Mountains in 1892 and again in 1903. Later, he became professor of Surveying and Geodesy at the University of Toronto.

## Ye Gods, Mr. MacCarthy!

Mt. Louis is a must ascent for every serious alpinist and its summit register reads like a who's who of the North American climbing establishment. The casual manner in which legendary guide Conrad Kain led Albert H. MacCarthy on the first ascent July 19, 1916, on a "day's picnic to view the scenery" required four hours of sustained climbing and has

Mt. Louis (left) and Mt. Fifi (right) from the Cascade Power Plant east of Banff

thighs until he extracted himself from his cramped quarters. MacCarthy soon followed and the two of them marched easily to the pointed summit where Kain let out a triumphant yodel to notify those in the valley below of their accomplishment.

Upon reaching the base of the mountain they both looked back at their accomplishment and Conrad uttered one of the most famous phrases in the history of Canadian mountaineering, "Ye Gods, Mr. MacCarthy, just look at that; they will never believe we climbed it."

## Mt. Edith 2554 m

Mt. Edith is an example of a dog-tooth mountain that consists of three separate summits; appropriately named South, Centre, and North Peaks. The peak was named after Mrs. Edith Orde (née Cox) who accompanied Lady Agnes Macdonald, the wife of Canada's first Prime Minister, on her trip to the Rocky Mountains in 1886.

J. Norman Collie and Fred Stephens first ascended North Peak (the highest summit of Mt. Edith) in 1900 via the west face. The climb necessitated the ascent of an interesting 18-m chimney, which subsequently led to the summit. Professor Collie wrote an amusing account of this ascent in the *Canadian Alpine Journal.* He had admired the peak from Banff and thought that it would be a good outing in which to initiate his good friend Fred Stephens to the enjoyment of climbing mountains. Fred had always protested that "climbing peaks, for

become one of the legends of the Rocky Mountains.

Kain was on a picnic in the company of Dr. and Mrs. W.E. Stone, along with Albert MacCarthy and his wife. While basking in the sunshine, admiring the dog-tooth peak, Kain began working out an imaginary line to its summit. It wasn't long before he and Mac-Carthy were scrambling up the mountain over ledges that flank its eastern face. They worked their way up complicated gullies and ribs until finally reaching a "truly wonderful chimney to delight the most exacting climber." It was just big enough to admit their shoulders with a slight squeeze. MacCarthy commented, "Here was a real chimney, the kind one speculates about but the like of which I never before had seen." The walls were entirely smooth, but Kain ascended the chimney with pressure holds using the palms of his hands, knees, and

Legendary Austrian guide Conrad Kain

North Pk.  Centre Pk.  South Pk.

the mere sake of climbing them, was foolishness — only, if sheep or goats could be shot by doing so, there might be some use in taking the trouble to get to the top of a mountain." Collie said he "looked forward to the pleasures of the initiated, when he should have Fred dangling on the end of an Alpine rope." Upon reaching the summit Collie stated, "Of course we built a cairn, after which Fred amused himself by hurling big stones down the cliffs — the only use he saw in such a mountain top was to pitch it over into the valley below."

## Mt. Cory 2802 m

Mt. Cory is a rather nondescript peak overlooking the Bow Valley that consists of two separate peaks identical in height. It was named in honour of William Wallace Cory (1865–1943), Deputy Minister of the Interior from 1905 to 1930. When viewed from the Trans-Canada Highway, the mountain appears to have three "rock ribs" that

William Wallace Cory

descend from its summit. However, perhaps the most distinguishing feature of the peak is the presence of a cave on its southwest side known as Hole-in-the-Wall. Even James Hector commented on this feature when he passed this way in 1858, and noted, "There are many caves in the limestone precipices of the Sawback Range, some of them at a great altitude above the valley." This landmark is best viewed from the Muleshoe picnic area, but a discerning eye can pick it out from the Trans-Canada Highway.

## Mt. Fifi 2621 m

In an act of complete disdain for rules of naming mountains, an unremarkable little dog belonging to Mrs. Edith Orde (see Mt. Edith, page 62) came to be glorified by having a mountain named in its honour. It is unclear whether or not Mrs. Orde and her dog "Fifi" hiked to the peak that would later bear Fifi's name, but one thing is certain, naming the

Left: Mt. Edith from the junction of the Bow Valley Parkway and the Trans-Canada Highway

Right: Hole-in-the-Wall from Muleshoe picnic area

Left: Lady
Aberdeen (neé
Ishbel Maria
Marjoribanks)

Right: The Finger

mountain after the dog defied all rules and seemed the ultimate gesture of "self-glorification." Is it any wonder that many consider the Canadian Rockies the worst named peaks in the world!

## The Finger 2545 m

This magnificent spire resembling a giant finger pointing to the sky is but a subsidiary spur of an unnamed peak (2800 m) east of this spire. Legend has it that the name of this pinnacle originated with the poem "David" by Earle Birney. Birney wrote this haunting, somewhat controversial poem about climbing and euthanasia in 1942 for which he received the first of his two Governor General awards. In Birney's poem, David is the source of the name:

*By the fading shreds of the
shattered storm clouds,
Lingering*

*There it was David who spied
to the south, remote*

*And unmapped, a sunlit spire
on Sawback, an overhang*

*Crooked like a talon.
David named it the Finger.*

This captivating poem, which should be on everyone's required list of reading, is of course completely fictional. In reality, Lawrence Grassi named the peak in 1935 and the name became official in 1967.

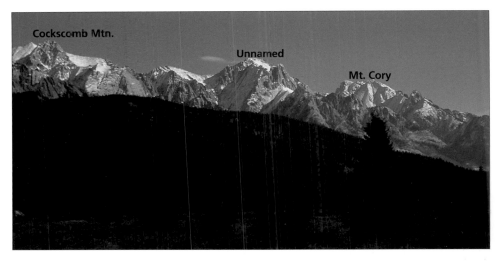

## Cockscomb Mtn. 2777 m

Whoever named this peak obviously thought the serrated summit resembled, you guessed it, a cocks comb.

## Mt. Ishbel 2908 m

The Sawback Range extends for over 9 km, ending at Mt. Ishbel the highest peak of the range at the extreme northern end of the range. Ishbel Maria Marjoribanks (1857–1939) was the daughter of the first Lord Tweedsmuir and the wife of the seventh Earl of Aberdeen (and so became Lady Aberdeen). She was a staunch advocate of women's rights and although she lived in Canada for only four years, while her husband was Governor General, she was the founding president and life-long patron of the National Council of Women of Canada. Lady Aberdeen also found time during her short stay in Canada to become a driving force behind the establishment of the Victorian Order of Nurses.

After returning to Great Britain, Lady Aberdeen and her husband occupied Haddo House, the family estate in Aberdeenshire where she

continued her humanitarian ways by helping to educate the children and servants of the tenant farmers at classes on Saturday night. Since young women were not allowed out in the evenings and could not attend these classes, she set up correspondence courses for the women.

Mt. Ishbel is not without its bit of controversy as there are some that insist that the peak was named for Ishbel MacDonald, the eldest daughter of Prime Minister Ramsay MacDonald of Great Britain, shortly after she had made a brief trip to the Rockies with her father.

**Top: Peaks of the Sawback Range from Moose Meadows**

**Bottom: Mt. Ishbel, the highest peak of the Sawback Range**

# The Massive Range

Mt. Brett    Massive Mtn.    Pilot Mtn.

Left: The Massive Range: "cubical blocks resembling bastions and towers"

Right: The Goat's Eye

Below: The famous tree trunk into which Sir George Simpson carved his and James Rowland's initials in 1841

The Massive Range consists of those mountains lying south and west of the Bow River along the Trans-Canada Highway. In 1841 Sir George Simpson was the first person of European descent to pass through this range. Simpson had recently been knighted and he was in such a rush in his journey around the world that he took little time to record his impressions of the magnificent scenery. He rushed past Cascade Mtn. and made his way to where Healy Creek joins the Bow River.

Alex Piché led Simpson up Healy Creek where Sir George observed that one of the peaks "presented a very peculiar feature in an opening of about eighty feet by fifty, which, at a distance, might have been taken for a spot of snow, but which, as we advanced nearer, assumed the appearance of the gateway of a giant's fortress." This natural hole in Eagle Mtn. is the famous landmark known to all skiers as "The Goat's Eye."

At the height of the land now bearing his name, Simpson was pleased to find some alpine heather that "appeared to me to be the very heather of the Highlands of Scotland," his ancestral home. He and Chief Factor James Rowland stayed just long enough at the pass to carve their initials and the year ("GS JR 1841") into a tree trunk to mark their passing.

Jim Brewster discovered this tree trunk over 60 years later, cut it out, and displayed it for years in his home in Banff. Today you can view this piece of history at the Banff Park Museum.

## Mt. Howard Douglas 2820 m

The mountain was named as a fitting tribute to Howard Douglas (1850–1929), the second superintendent of Rocky Mountains Park. He is remembered as a wildlife conservationist and "visionary" park superintendent. Howard Douglas was a Calgary coal merchant, appointed to the position of superintendent by the Liberal government to replace Charles Stewart after the fall of the Conservative government in the general election of 1896. Douglas would become known for two legendary achievements: spearheading the protection of the natural resources (including the wildlife) in the newly formed park and instituting the "warden system."

Douglas became a staunch "conservationist" who quickly recognized the value of the natural resources of

Mt. Howard Douglas      Eagle Mtn.

the park to its survival. In an effort to protect the wildlife, Douglas lobbied the government to increase the size of Rocky Mountains Park to an astounding 12,500 km² (4900 mi.² and sought to eliminate illegal hunting and poaching within park boundaries. The immense size of the park created problems, with Douglas commenting, "I find great difficulty in enforcing the laws ... as game is generally killed in the more remote districts, and offenders are careful to see that their actions are unobserved." In an effort to suppress this illegal hunting, he mounted a campaign to institute a full-time game warden service. In 1909 he supervised the implementation of his vision when Howard Sibbald became the first Chief Game Warden, a post he would head for 25 years.

Perhaps Douglas's greatest achievement, however, began in 1898 with the building of an animal paddock whose purpose was to conserve and protect the all but extinct plains buffalo. Donations to the pro-

**Howard Douglas**

gram increased the size of the herd until, by 1906, "Buffalo Paddock" had become home to 51 beasts. But Douglas wasn't finished yet, and in 1905 began lobbying the government to purchase the largest remaining herd of buffalo in North America, owned by Michel Pablo on the Flathead Reservation in Montana. It took Pablo five years to round up all the buffalo, but by 1912 the entire herd of 703 animals had found new homes either at Buffalo National Park near Wainwright, Alberta, or at Elk Island National Park east of Edmonton.

Mt. Howard Douglas and Eagle Mtn. from the junction of the Bow Valley Parkway with the Trans-Canada Highway

## Eagle Mtn. 2820 m

Although uncertainty surrounds who named the mountain, it is obvious that the source of the name was the magnificent bird of prey.

## Mt. Bourgeau 2930 m

"Looking up the valley to the N.S.W. we had before us a truncated mountain, entirely composed of massive horizontal strata, and which I named Mount Bourgeau." This was

Mt.Brett  Massive Mtn.  Pilot Mtn.

Left: Mt. Bourgeau from Vermilion Lakes

Right: Peaks of the Massive Range

the first landmark named by James Hector in the upper part of the Bow Valley and he named the peak after his botanical companion Eugène Bourgeau.

Bourgeau was born in 1813 in the little village of Brizon, high in the French Swiss Alps. His interest in alpine plants led to his specialization in the subject, earning the diminutive botanist many honours and glowing tributes in the process. He was often referred to as the "Prince of Botanical Collectors" and jumped at the opportunity to be added to the expedition's scientific contingent.

Bourgeau may have been an excellent botanist, but Palliser exclaimed that "he was a shocking horseman, his legs were so short, and the fact that he was a good sailor did not help him on the prairies." He spoke not a

Eugène Bourgeau, the "Prince of Botanical Collectors"

word of English, but despite all of his shortcomings, Palliser heaped praise on the his botanist, exclaiming that "he has been a most active energetic and excellent companion, always hard at work in which his whole soul seems engrossed and no matter what his fatigues or privations may be his botanical specimens are always his first care … He is most indefatigable and always at work." Through his efforts, over 60,000 plants were collected, identified, and preserved by the Palliser Expedition, including 50 varieties of alpine plants that Bourgeau himself collected at an elevation of over 2400 m.

## Mt. Brett 2984 m

Mt. Brett was named in honour of one of Banff's true icons, The Honourable Dr. Robert G. Brett, who served as Lieutenant-Governor of Alberta from 1915 to 1925. Dr. Brett (1851–1929) was born in Strathroy, Ontario and received his Doctor of Medicine degree from the University of Toronto. During World War I he served as an honourary colonel of the Eighty-second Battalion of the Canadian Expeditionary Force. After practising medicine in Ontario from 1874 to 1879, he finally came west to Manitoba in 1880 where he became one of the founders of the Manitoba Medical College. His fortunes were to forever change when he moved to Banff in 1883.

Politically astute, Brett was elected a member of the Legislative Assembly of the North-West Territories in 1888 for the electoral district of Red Deer. Thereafter, he became a virtually unstoppable political force running under the banner of the Conservative Party. He was re-elected by acclamation in 1891 for Banff and again in 1894. Initially defeated in the election of 1898, Brett won re-election on the basis of a judicial recount and remained in office as the official Leader of the Opposition until his retirement in 1901. Brett was always a staunch advocate of reform in the management of Banff National Park and was responsible in 1896 for proposing that the District of Alberta become an autonomous province.

Effective October 20, 1915, on the advice of Prime Minister Sir Robert Borden, Dr. Robert G. Brett was appointed Lieutenant-Governor of Alberta by the Governor General of Canada, his Royal Highness The Duke of Connaught. He served in that capacity until 1925. Dr. Brett died on September 16, 1929 in Calgary and is interred in the Banff Cemetery.

## Massive Mtn. 2436 m

This mountain is neither massive nor tall. It is exceeded in elevation by all the peaks that surround it, so if

Pilot Mtn., from the east at Sawback viewpoint

you are confused why a diminutive peak such as this was named "Massive" you are not alone!

## Pilot Mtn. 2935 m

Dr. George Mercer Dawson named this peak in 1884 because it is visible for long distances down the Bow Valley and served as a landmark for approaching exploration parties. This mountain looks entirely different depending on the direction from which it is viewed (see photo, page 66), but by far the most impressive view is from the north.

## Copper Mtn. 2795 m

Botanist John Macoun (1831–1920), the "Father of Canadian Botany," named this mountain in 1884 while botanizing in the area. He named the mountain after reports of copper and silver deposits had been "discovered" on the slopes of the peak by Joe Healy and J.S. Dennis in 1881. Edwin Hunter, a Stoney also know as "Gold Seeker," led them to this mountain where they were shown some minor deposits containing "copper ore." Subsequent analysis later determined the deposits to be

Copper Mtn.

that is exactly what James Hector thought when he described the scene in his journal entry of August 17, 1858. Over a quarter of century later, Sir Sandford Fleming also commented on the uniqueness of this mountain: "Westward we see Castle Mountain to our right. The resemblance to Cyclopean masonry has doubtless suggested the name, for it is marked by huge masses of castellated-looking work, with turreted flanks." Was there ever a more appropriate name for a mountain? Little did Hector realize when he named this mountain that it would become the centre of a controversy that would rage for over 30 years.

During a visit to Canada by General Dwight D. Eisenhower in January 1946, it was decided to rename Castle Mountain in honour of the Allied commander in chief during World War II. The gesture was to act "as a lasting expression of the high admiration and esteem ... " in which General Eisenhower was held by the people of Canada. And so, by direct order of then Prime Minister Mackenzie King, in a willful abuse of political power and disdain for historical context, Castle Mtn. was erased by the stroke of a pen.

The resentment on both sides of the border was both predictable and warranted, but it would be over 30 years before, in 1979, public pressure would result in the mountain reverting to its original and logical name. Eisenhower Tower was reserved for the name of the prominent pinnacle (2751 m) at the southeast end of the mountain.

nothing more than sulfides of lead, but this did not stop a flood of prospectors to the area in 1883 with dreams of discovering a motherlode of copper and silver (see Silver City, page 73).

## Castle Mtn. 2766 m

If you could view Castle Mtn. massif from the air you would see that the mountain forms a gigantic U shape as it bends around to join Helena Ridge (2862 m) to the east. Between the two lie a glorious alpine valley and two exquisite mountain tarns. You would also notice that Castle Mtn. itself is not the highest peak of the massif. That honour belongs to Stuart Knob (2850 m), about 3 km north of the "Castle."

### The Naming Controversy

"Seeming to stand out in the centre of the valley is a very remarkable mountain, still at a distance of 12 miles, which looks exactly like a gigantic castle." Castle Mtn. commands the entire Bow Valley and

Castle Mtn.

Eisenhower Pk.

## Geological Significance

Castle Mtn. belongs to the Main Ranges of the Rocky Mountains and is a significant geological feature of the Canadian Rockies. Castle Mtn. Fault was formed when Pre-Cambrian rock (400–600 million years old) was thrust up and over much younger rock (200 million years old). These rock formations are the oldest known in the Canadian Rockies. It is also significant to note that Castle Mtn. is at the junction between the Main Ranges and the Front Ranges of the Rockies.

In 1911 Professor A.P. Coleman proposed the interesting theory that Castle Mtn. was once joined to Copper Mtn., 10 km across the valley. In *The Canadian Rockies: New and Old Trails,* he states that the "innocent-looking Bow and its tributaries, helped by weather, frost, and glaciers, have actually destroyed and swept away to build up the plains from the many cubic miles of rock that once joined the two peaks."

## First Ascent

Sir James Hector and his assistant Robert Sutherland attempted to climb Castle Mtn. on August 19, 1858, but after a tedious hike through the woods they were only able to ascend about 600 m above the valley floor. After emerging from the trees they "passed round to the N. side of the mountain, and found that a deep valley separated it from a lower spur composed of splintery shale of a dull red colour." They became the first white people to view Helena Ridge, Rockbound Lake, and Tower Lake in the huge U-shaped amphitheatre behind the mountain.

In 1886 Professor A.P. Coleman, with a prospector from Silver City known only as "Mose," completed the first ascent of Castle Mtn. via today's popular scramble route on the backside of the peak. Today's scramblers may find Coleman's description of the ascent amusing:

Castle Mtn. from the Bow River at Castle junction

Castle Mtn.  Eisenhower Pk.  Helena Ridge

Top: Castle Mtn. (left), Eisenhower Tower, and Helena Ridge (right), from Moose Meadows viewpoint

Bottom: Protection Mtn.

*Some of the climbing was quite risky work, since the projecting knobs of rock were often loose, and gave way under the hand or foot. Above the edge of the cliff, however, going was easy, so that the highest part of the Castle (nine thousand feet) was not hard to reach, and the wonderful view of the Bow River, four thousand feet below, was quite worth seeing.*

### Home of the Chinook Wind?

There is a legend among the Stoneys that Castle Mtn. is the home of the Chinook Wind. The following is adapted from *Indian Legends of the Northern Rockies*. Many, many moons ago, as the tale goes, a great battle of the winds took place in the mountains. The fierce and evil North Wind had seen the lovely South Wind playing with her little daughter, Chinook Wind, and swept down to carry her away. Seeing their plight, the strong West Wind flew to their assistance, but in the ensuing struggle, little Chinook Wind became blinded. Since she could no longer see to fly great distances, she was given a home close to the foothills and prairies on Castle Mtn. On spring nights when a gentle and warm wind blows out to the prairies melting the snow, they say it is the little blind Chinook Wind stealing down from Castle Mtn. to look for her lost mother and leaving spring behind her wherever she goes.

## Protection Mtn. 2786 m and 2970 m

James F. Porter named this mountain in 1911, although it is unclear why he gave it that name. This massif, which is approximately 10 km in length, separates Wonder Valley to the east from the valley of Baker Creek, and whether or not that had anything to do with the name given by Porter is uncertain. There are actually two high points on this peak; the northwest high point is 2786 m while the southeast high point (unofficially called Television Peak because of the repeater station on top) is 2970 m.

# Silver City

The Bow Valley adjacent to Castle Mtn. was once the site of a mining fraud and scandal surpassed only by the infamous Bre-X gold mining scandal more than 100 years later. In this case the scandal was perpetuated by the "discovery" in 1881 of copper and silver deposits, on what would later become Copper Mtn., by two Americans from Montana, Joe Healy and J.S. Dennis. Joe Healy had the samples assayed by a friend in Montana and the "positive results" of copper and silver in the ore samples (later to be shown to be nothing more than sulfides of lead) elicited a great deal of excitement. By 1883 Joe Healy and his brother John had raised enough capital from investors to begin mining operations at Copper Mtn.

Prospectors seeking their fortune began flooding into the region and by 1883 it is estimated that more than 3000 silver-hungry prospectors began staking their claims in the valley. Businesses quickly began to spring up to cater to their needs. Prospectors could choose between the Queens, Castle Park Hotel, the Miner's Home, or various other rooming houses for cheap accommodation. Some just pitched tents or built their own crude shacks on the slopes of Castle Mtn. A general store, restaurants, and saloons catered to other needs, while gambling dens could be found at the rear of most establishments. It didn't take long for Silver City to gain an unsavoury "rip-roaring" reputation. The law was pretty lax and eventually the North West Mounted Police was sent in to prevent complete deterioration into complete lawlessness.

Top: Silver City in its heyday

Bottom: The remains of a prospector's cabin on the lower slopes of Castle Mtn.

Joe Smith in front of his cabin complex at Silver City

In 1884 Silver City's bubble burst as mines failed and dreams of discovering huge deposits didn't "pan out." Joseph Healy was even forced to admit that there hadn't been sufficient ore uncovered to warrant financial backing for projects in the region. By the fall of 1884 Silver City had disappeared as fast as it had arisen. Reverend William Spotswood Green paid a visit to Silver City in 1888 and recounted that after "throwing down our packs near the railway station we walked off to explore the 'City.' There was a marvelous stillness about it; no sign of any living thing. We reached the grass-grown street, and looking into the empty houses heard no sound but the flapping of torn paper, which once bedizened the walls." Eventually nearly all of the wood used to construct the town was removed and used in the construction of the new town of Banff. All that was left in the meadow below the slopes of Castle Mtn. were stories of fraud, scandal, lost fortunes, and interesting characters.

## Old Joe Smith

Old Joe Smith was one of those legendary characters that remained in Silver City long after its demise. Originally from Montreal, Smith began his migration west while working for the CPR. He quit the CPR and went to Silver City in 1883 with dreams of finding a motherlode and becoming rich. He built a rooming house with a pool hall where he sold watches, shoelaces, and buttons to the patrons in order to make ends meet. Old Joe never did find his motherlode but he remained in the area for more than 50 years, hunting and trapping. Eventually as Old Joe's eyesight waned and he became blind, friends from Banff had him moved to the Lacombe Home in Calgary where he died shortly afterwards in 1937.

Although there was never enough precious metal found to justify full-scale mining operations, two mine-shafts were begun; one called "Alberta Mine" on Copper Mtn. and the other named "The Queen of the Hills" on the slopes of Castle Mtn. Rumours of huge "strikes" attracted not only prospectors but also other entrepreneurs intent on getting rich not from the ore but from the pockets of the prospectors. Stories of fraud began to emerge and some suggested that samples had been "salted" in order that certain "entrepreneurial types" could float stock, sell quickly, reap huge profits, and disappear before their schemes were uncovered.

# Park Prisoners

In 1915 Nick Olnyk, Park Prisoner No. 98, wrote a letter to his wife in which he commented on his plight in the camp saying, "the conditions here are very poor, so that we cannot go on much longer. We are not getting enough to eat. We are hungry as dogs. They are sending us to work as they don't believe us and we are very weak." Such was the predicament of some of Canada's "enemy aliens" during World War I, in what can be described as the darkest days in the history of Banff National Park.

It all started when Canada entered World War I in 1914. Suddenly the hopes and dreams of thousands of people who had immigrated to Canada at the turn of the 20th century were shattered when the government required over 88,000 emigrants from countries with which we were at war to register as "enemy aliens."

Paranoia regarding security gripped Canadians and this "anti-alien" sentiment resulted in the establishment of 24 internment camps across the country under provisions of the War Measures Act. Most of these "foreign nationals" were unemployed victims of the 1913 depression and came from all walks of life, but fully two-thirds of them were of Ukrainian descent. One of these camps, deemed "Castle Camp," was set up at the foot of Castle Mtn. near the former site of Silver City.

Major-General Sir William Otter, Director of Canadian Internment Operations, and J.B. Harkin, Dominion Parks Commissioner, met in Banff to discuss the internment of so-called "undesirables" and to provide cheap labour for park projects. At the time, Harkin was preoccupied

Park prisoners constructing the Banff-Laggan highway

Top: Castle Camp

Bottom: Ukrainian memorial to internees on the Bow Valley Parkway

with road building in the national parks and he jumped at the opportunity to carry out these projects with little cost to the government. The men who were made available were technically prisoners of war, but in reality the majority of internees were unemployed or destitute "aliens" of Ukrainian, Austrian, and Hungarian ancestry. Under the terms of the agreement, the Militia Department would supply the internment guard, while the parks branch would house the men and select work projects. Camp internees were expected to work a six-day week at the rate of 25¢ per day.

By July 19, 1916 as many as 600 prisoners and 182 guards occupied Castle Camp. The internees' new home was a large canvas camp within a 110-by-220 m stockade, surrounded by a 3 m barbed wire fence, in a clearing that had recently been destroyed by fire. The plan of park authorities was to have the internees complete the road from Banff to Lake Louise. Before the end of the summer, park prisoners had cleared 6.5 km of the new road to Laggan and this, it might be noted, was accomplished using only picks, shovels, and wheelbarrows.

The following year, prisoners completed the roadway to the upper hot springs, made improvements to the Lake Minnewanka road, and cleared some right-of-way for the road to Sundance Canyon.

At the end of July 1917, the camps were closed, but the blemish of their existence will forever blot the history of Banff National Park.

# The Secret of the Sacred Soils

The red ochre deposits near Vermilion Pass had been a prized item of trade for the Kootenay Indians for many generations. These deposits were considered to be sacred soils. On August 21, 1858 James Hector was about to become the first white man to view these sacred soils. Nimrod, his Stoney guide, led Hector to the deposits by following an ancient Kootenay trail across the Pass from the Bow Valley. The following legend has been adapted from "The Stonies of Alberta" and is based on a narrative by Jonas Dixon.

In the beginning, Waka Taga (Great Mystery), Mu (Spirit of Thunder), Macoyah Debe (Little People), and Waheambah (Sun) created four sacred soils from the first waters and mud pools of Mother Earth. Each soil had great powers and possessed a powerful medicine.

The most sacred of the four soils is the White Soil made by Waka Taga. White Soil is a fire-soil person who lives in a lodge in the muskeg country and his brother is the fierce North Wind. Green Soils are made by the Macoyah Debe and Grandmother Earth. These soils are the persons of greenness and growth and their lodges are in the big country where the hills roll towards the aspen. Black Soils are made by Mu from the powder left by lightning when the eyes of Mu pierce the sky. These soils are very powerful and have the power to "bury weakness, [and] bury disease." Red Soils are made by Waheambah. "These are the brown, dark brown, and blood soil [of the Stoney] nation. These yield life-strength of blood." Red soil man makes his lodge on the high prairies where his brothers come to visit him often as drought and cracked-earth skin.

The Macoyah Debe have been given the power to rule over the four sacred soils of the earth. The Little People sit inside the soils as medicine-watchers. They bring the soil-medicines up from their subterranean world and leave them in special places where the Stoneys can find them. Stoney spirit men and women hold the secrets to the medicinal power of the sacred soils and are the source of the great powers of Stoney medicine.

The four soil-medicines are used in spiritual painting and speak of prophecies. It is said that when spirit people use these soils for rock painting, shield painting, or skin painting, the soil spirit penetrates the surfaces and even when the paint fades or washes from the skin, the medicine of the soil still remains

"Only a spirit man or woman may use these sacred soil medicines, which are made sacred by the sacred ones to serve the people."

Ochre springs: "Where the red clay spirit is taken."

# Vermilion Pass

The summit of Vermilion Pass (1651m) is the dividing line between the waters of the Vermilion River (a tributary of the Kootenay River) flowing west to the Pacific Ocean and Altrude Creek (a tributary of the Bow River) flowing east to Hudson Bay. The first recorded crossing of the pass by a person of European descent was in

1858 by James Hector, but it is obvious that the route over the pass had been used by many generations of the Kootenay in search of the red iron oxides found at the mineral springs on the western side of the pass. The deposits from these ochre beds are the source of the name of the pass.

Early on the morning of August 20, 1858, James Hector forded the Bow River and began an

**Stark grandeur at Vermilion Pass**

arduous ascent through deadfall to Vermilion Pass. Hector describes the ascent in detail:

*At first we had a tough climb up the face of a terrace of loose shingle for 150 feet, but going a little round we might have ascended it where less steep. We at first followed the brink of the valley, which the creek has cut through these superficial deposits. We then struck through the wood to the south-west, which clothe the gentle sloping and wide valley that leads to the height of land ... We had been travelling six hours through the woods when we came to the height of land, but had not made more than 12 miles.*

Hector had "discovered" what would later be called Vermilion Pass as his guide Nimrod had led him over an ancient trade route the Kootenay had used for generations. Today's visitor will not find the going as tortuous as Hector did in 1858.

# At the Great Divide

Hector camped at the pass just above present-day Altrude Lakes and noted:

*The valley at this point is several miles wide, and the mountains on either hand are still wooded a long way up the slope. The source of the stream [Altrude Creek] flowing to the east is from a deep lake [one of the Altrude Lakes] with rocky margins ... A stream of muddy water, about 12 feet broad, descends from the north-west, and when within 300 yards of this lake turns off to the southwest, forming the first water we had seen flowing to the Pacific.*

Hector was at The Great Divide and made a special note of the

Stanley Pk.

## The Vermilion Pass Burn

Left: Stanley Pk. and Altrude Lakes from Vista Lake viewpoint

Right: The Great Divide at Vermilion Pass

"dividing of the waters."

It is not clear why Nimrod chose the Vermilion Pass route for James Hector instead of continuing to follow the Bow River up the valley. We will probably never know for certain, but it seems likely that Hector was in fact searching for a pass that could serve as a major transportation route and was following a crude map sketched on a piece of bark by a Stoney. In 1913 the Boundary Commission alludes to this fact, stating that "the Vermilion Pass is the first pass southeast of the Kicking Horse Pass suitable for a main line of travel across the range."

In 1912 CPR engineer Robert Bruce proposed the construction of an all-weather road from Banff over the Vermilion Pass to Windermere, B.C., following almost exactly the route taken by Hector in 1858. Construction of the Banff–Windermere Highway began in 1914 but economic problems delayed completion of the roadway until the fall of 1922.

No doubt you have wondered why the trees along the highway appear much younger than those in the Bow Valley. Look more closely, and you will notice the charred spars of the old forest on the slopes of the mountains in the pass. The new growth you are witnessing is the result of fire caused by a lightning strike on the slopes of Mt. Whymper on July 9, 1968. Fanned by strong winds, the fire grew rapidly and burned out of control for three days. On the fourth day, firefighters were aided in their struggle to control the blaze by welcome rain. The fire was finally extinguished on July 18. After the smoke cleared, it was determined that the fire had consumed over 2950 ha of virgin subalpine forest. It is now generally recognized that fire plays an essential role in forest succession, as mineral-rich ash is recycled back into the ecosystem. No sooner had the ground cooled than the forest was reborn in a flush of nutrients released by the ash. Nearly all of the new growth you see is lodgepole pine (*Pinus contorta* var. *latifolia*), a fire successional conifer. Just as quick to colonize the denuded landscape is another fire successional plant, *Epilobium angustifolium*, or as most people know it, fireweed.

# The Legend of the Fireweed

Common fireweed
with Mt. Whymper
in the background

The following native legend has been adapted from *Old Man's Garden* by Annora Brown:

During a battle between warring tribes a young brave was captured and was scheduled to be tortured by his enemies. A young Indian maiden, in love with the captured brave, could not bear to see him tortured to death and set fire to the far end of the camp as a diversion in order to rescue her lover. As her enemies fought the fire, she untied her lover and they fled into the forest. When her enemies realized what she had done they gave chase. The Great Spirit took pity on the brave maiden and wherever her moccasins touched the ground, great flames arose. These flames soon turned her pursuers back and eventually the flames turned into the brilliant coloured flowers of the fireweed.

# Usna Waki-Cagubi: "Where the red clay spirit is taken"

On, August 21, 1858, Hector continued his journey and descended into the valley of the Vermilion River. Four hours later he reached the source of the ochre the Kootenay used as an item of trade:

*In the corner of the valley on the right side, is the Vermilion Plains, which is about a mile in extent, with a small stream flowing through it. Its surface is entirely covered with yellow ochre, washed down from the ferruginous shales in the mountains. The Kootanie Indians come to this place sometimes, and we found the remains of a camp and of a large fire which they had used to convert the ochre into the red oxide which they take away to trade to the Indians of the low country, and also to the Blackfeet as a pigment, calling it vermilion.*

Red ochre or, more specifically hydrate of iron (III) oxide ($Fe_2O_3H_2O$ is a yellowish to red coloured clay formed by the saturation of the clay with iron-rich water. To native peoples, red was a sacred colour with great power. It signified blood, strength, success, and spiritual protection. Red was also symbolic of war, hence its use as a war paint. The Kootenay "mined"

the clay at the Paint Pots. By heating the clay to various temperatures they could alter the colour from yellow through red to brown. The pulverized clay was then mixed with oil or grease and was used to colour pottery, leather, the body, or even rock.

# Peaks of the Ball Range

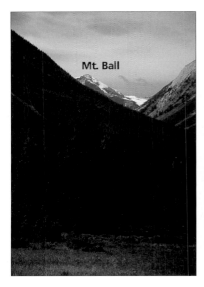

Mt. Ball

Stanley Pk.

The Ball Range is bounded on the southwest by the Vermilion River and on the northeast by the Bow River. Principle peaks of this range form part of the Continental Divide.

## Mt. Ball 3311 m

James Hector named the range and mountain in honour of John Ball (1818–1889), although there is some confusion as to which peak Hector was actually referring to. On August 18, while still in the Bow Valley, Hector wrote, "Soon after starting this morning we came to a hill, about 400 feet high, from which I took a set

of bearings and got a fine view of the mountains. Through a deep valley to the southwest is a very massive mountain, completely snow capped." Hillsdale Meadows viewpoint on the Bow Valley Parkway is the only place you can glimpse the massive, snow-capped Mt. Ball.

John Ball was a very close friend of Captain John Palliser and was influential in securing government support for Palliser's expedition. Born in Dublin and educated at Cambridge, Ball was a student of mathematics, meteorology, botany, and mountain glaciology. He became the first president of the

Left: Mt. Ball from Hillsdale Meadows viewpoint on the Bow Valley Parkway

Right: Stanley Peak from Highway 93

Storm Mtn.

Storm Mtn. from
Castle Junction

Alpine Club and author of *The Alpine Guide*. Ball was elected a member of the British parliament in 1852 and was under-secretary of state for the colonies from 1855 to 1857.

## Storm Mtn. 3161 m

Geologist Dr. George Mercer Dawson named two peaks in the Rocky Mountains "Storm"; one in the Highwood Pass of Kananaskis Country and this peak on the Continental Divide. He apparently named both peaks for the same reason — a propensity for storms about their summits. Legend has it that pioneer packers used the peak in the Bow Valley to forecast the weather.

Lord Stanley

## Stanley Pk. 3155 m

During one of his excursions to the Canadian Alps in 1901, Sir Edward Whymper named this peak in honour of Sir Frederick Arthur Stanley (1841–1908), the sixth Governor General of Canada. Edward Whymper was 62 years of age when his entourage of crack Swiss guides led him to the summit of this virgin peak in 1901.

Lord Stanley served as Governor General from 1888 to 1893, after which he returned to England where, as the 16th Earl of Derby, he became the Lord Mayor of Liverpool and the First Chancellor of the University of Liverpool.

Lord Stanley travelled widely while in Canada and was an avid outdoorsman, but Canadians will best remember him for donating the Stanley Cup, the most prestigious trophy in professional hockey. He originally donated the trophy in 1893 as an award for Canada's top-ranking amateur hockey club, but since 1926 it has come to symbolize the championship of the National Hockey League. In recognition of this and for his love of outdoor sports, Lord Stanley was inducted into the Canadian Hockey Hall of Fame in 1945 in the "Honoured Builders" category.

# Peaks of the Bow Range

## Boom Mtn. 2760 m

The Great Divide and the boundary between Banff and Kootenay National Parks both run along the crest of the ridge that forms Boom Mtn. Nestled between Boom Mtn. and Mt. Bell is a beautiful valley containing Boom Lake. Walter Wilcox explored the valley and lake in the 1890s and his description of the surroundings is probably the origin of this unusual name. Wilcox provided the following account:

> This lake runs about north-west and south-east and sends a stream into the Vermilion Pass. It is about a half mile wide and probably three miles in length. One of its most curious features is a crescent-shaped dam of logs and tree roots about one mile from the lower end ... I thought at first of naming the lake from this circumstance. but was unable to make anything euphonious out of "log-dammed lake."

Loggers refer to a dam formed from drifted wood as a "boom", so that is perhaps the explanation. Another possible scenario is that the name originated from the "booming" sound made by avalanches as they thundered down from the slopes of the mountains encircling the lake. Numerous avalanche paths in the valley attest to the frequency of such events.

Top: Peaks around Boom Lake viewed from Moose Meadows

Bottom: View west from Castle Junction

Mt. Bell

Panorama Ridge

## Chimney Pk. 3000 m

Chimney Pk. is about 3 km west of Boom Mtn. on the Great Divide. A glacier draping the west side of this peak is the ultimate source of the Vermilion River, which flows west to the Pacific Ocean. This peak apparently received its named from a prominent wide crack, (or "chimney" as alpinists call it), which was used by E.O. Wheeler and T.G. Longstaff during their first ascent of the mountain in 1910.

## Mt. Bell 2910 m

Mt. Bell was named to honour Dr. Frederick Charles Bell (1883–1971), one of the founding members of the Alpine Club of Canada and president of the club from 1926 to 1928. Doctor Bell was a ship's surgeon for the CPR and Chief Medical Officer for Veterans Affairs in British Columbia. According to *The Rocky Mountains of Canada South,* Dr. Bell originally, "called this mountain Bellevue but the name was shortened in view of the fact that his sister, Nora, was a member of what may have been the first ascent party."

## Mt. Whymper 2845 m

Mt. Whymper is a minor peak named in honour of the famous British alpinist and "Conqueror of the Matterhorn," Sir Edward Whymper (1840–1911). The peak, which looms above Vermilion Pass, lies entirely within Kootenay National Park but is included here for two reasons. First, it is viewed annually by thousands of travellers on the Banff–Windermere Highway, and second, it was named after one of the most famous mountaineers in history.

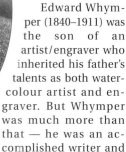

Edward Whymper

Edward Whymper (1840–1911) was the son of an artist/engraver who inherited his father's talents as both watercolour artist and engraver. But Whymper was much more than that — he was an accomplished writer and speaker, a self-taught scientist, and perhaps the greatest mountain climber of his time. Although his exploits as a climber span the globe, he will be forever remembered for his famous or "infamous," depending on your point of view, conquest of the Matterhorn.

The Matterhorn had repelled all attempts by the leading climbers of the day and had thwarted Whymper on seven previous attempts. Finally, in 1863, Whymper "conquered" the peak. What followed was a story of conquest, jubilation, tragedy, disbelief, and later, unfounded accusations of misdeeds. It was a horrific, yet riveting experience as Whymper watched four of his companions hurtle into oblivion when their rope snapped as they descended from the summit. The picture is one that would haunt Whymper for the rest of his life, even to his deathbed. Just prior to his death a leading English newspaper reported that Whymper uttered:

Mt. Whymper

> *I am seventy-two and I am finished ... every right, do you understand, I see my comrades on the Matterhorn slipping on their backs, their arms outstretched, one after the other, in perfect order at equal distances — Croz, the guide, first; then Hadow, then Hudson, and lastly Douglas. Yes I shall always see them slipping in order on their backs with their hands turned back, and I shall never see Zermatt again, where I spent my most ardent hours, nor my Matterhorn.*

Perhaps indulging in prodigious quantities of "spirits" was Whymper's attempt to erase this horrific event from his memory.

Whymper made a number of excursions to the Canadian Alps at the turn of the 20th century as a guest of the Canadian Pacific Railway. Some even regard these visits as a turning point in the history of Canadian mountaineering. Others regard the visits as nothing more than a promotional stunt on behalf of the CPR that involved a pompous, arrogant, and aging mountaineer with a serious drinking problem.

His trip to the Rockies in 1901 created quite a stir. When word that four notable Swiss guides were to accompany Whymper, rumours immediately began to circulate that he was after the virgin summit of Mt. Assiniboine, the "Matterhorn of the Rockies." Only the proud and arrogant Whymper knew otherwise. Why would he risk his reputation with failure on this magnificent peak? After all, he was now 62 years old, and advancing age and hard drinking had conspired against such a lofty ambition.

With his entourage of Swiss guides and ever present cases of liquor, Whymper made a number of first ascents during his visit of 1901, including that of the mountain that was named in his honour. Though considerably past his prime, Whymper was considered by his colleagues and Swiss guides as one "tough son of a bitch".

Top: Mt. Whymper from the Stanley Glacier trail

Bottom: Whymper's legacy?

# The Lake of Little Fishes:
## *Ho Run Num Nay*

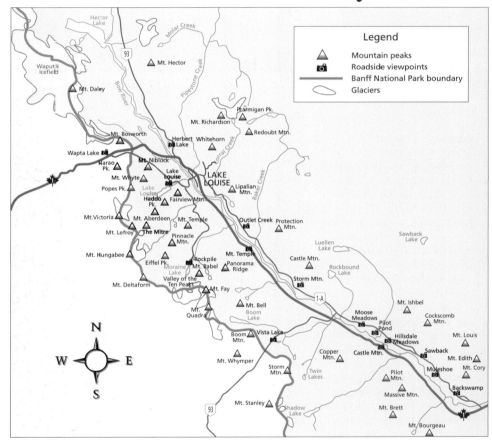

**Legend**

⛰ Mountain peaks
📷 Roadside viewpoints
— Banff National Park boundary
⬭ Glaciers

**Illustrated map of the peaks and viewpoints in the vicinity of Lake Louise**

As God is my judge I never in all my explorations saw such a matchless scene. On the right and the left forests that had never known the axe came down to the shores apparently growing out of the blue and green waters. The background, a mile and a half away, was divided into three tones of white, opal and brown where the glacier ceased and merged with the shining water. The sun, high in the noon-hour, poured into the pool, which reflected the whole landscape that formed the horseshoe.

Tom Wilson reminiscing in *England and Canada, A Summer Tour Between Old and New Westminster*

# Discovering a Gem

erhaps Wilson was contemplating his original thoughts as he sat beside the shore of his discovery and said, "For some time [we] sat and smoked and gazed at the gem of beauty beneath the glacier. I called the beautiful sheet of water before me 'Emerald Lake' and under that name it appeared on the first geological map ever made of the Canadian Rockies in that region."

Since time immemorial avalanches have thundered down the slopes of Mt. Victoria and for thousands of years the sound would seem to have fallen on deaf ears; that is, not until Tom Wilson, a packer for the CPR, heard these thunderous roars while sitting around the campfire one rainy evening in 1882. He inquired of Edwin Hunter (Gold Seeker of Copper Mtn. fame) as to the origin of the noise and was told it originated on a mountain above the lake known to the Stoney people as *Ho run num nay* or the "Lake of Little Fishes." It is also said that Wilson enhanced the tale for a gullible public by insisting that Edwin Hunter said that the thunder emanated from a place "where the blue picture is painted; the picture that the Great Spirit made for the Indians. White man's pictures always fade, Indian's picture lasts forever." The next day began wet and miserable, so Wilson delayed his trip to Kicking Horse Pass and persuaded Edwin Hunter to lead him to the "spot where God made thunder, and painted indelible,

Top: The Lake of Little Fishes

Bottom: Tom Wilson (ca. 1920s) beside Lake Louise

permanent masterpieces." When they reached the shore of the lake Wilson was completely awestruck and is said to have uttered the words quoted at the beginning of this chapter. If indeed, there ever was a masterpiece painted by the hand of God, then surely Lake Louise must be that magnum opus.

# It Had To Be a Royal Name

**Princess Louise Caroline Alberta**

Wilson originally named the lake Emerald Lake, so what of the name "Louise"? According to Robert E. Campbell, who worked as a packer for Wilson, it was Wilson himself who was responsible for the name change. In 1884 Wilson accompanied Sir Richard Temple and his lovely daughter (coincidentally named Louise) to the lake and "seeing the powder blue hues of the silt-laden waters, renamed his 'Emerald' lake 'Louise'."

Officially, the source of the name is P.K. Hindman, an assistant of Major Rogers who in 1886 renamed Wilson's Emerald Lake in honour of Princess Louise Caroline Alberta, the wife of the Marquis of Lorne, Governor General of Canada and the granddaughter of King George III.

Princess Louise Caroline Alberta was born at Buckingham Palace on March 18, 1848, the fourth daughter and sixth child of nine children born to Queen Victoria and Prince Albert. She was beautiful and intelligent, with no small talent as an artist and sculptor, but Queen Victoria described her as "dreadfully contradictory, very indiscreet and from that making mischief frequently." She was, to be quite blunt, a "different princess," not overly fond of stuffy royal ceremony. As if to prove her point, in 1868, at the age of 22 she became engaged to John Douglas Southerland Campbell, Marquis of Lorne, and the eldest son of the Duke of Argyll. This caused quite stir because in the 19th century British royals did not marry "commoners," despite the Marquis being a distant descendent of the kings of Scotland. Nonetheless, the couple survived the turmoil and married in St. George's Chapel at Windsor Castle on March 21, 1871.

The Marquis was a member of British parliament when Prime Minister Benjamin Disraeli persuaded Queen Victoria to appoint him Governor General of Canada. It was an office he would hold from October 15, 1878 until 1883. During this tenure, the Marquis and his wife Princess Louise were instrumental in the founding of the Royal Canadian Academy of the Arts (which formed the foundation of the National Gallery of Canada) and the Royal Society of Canada, a literary and scientific academy.

In 1882 after much lobbying by the Marquis of Lorne, the Prime Minister named the new district of Alberta after the Princess. In 1889 majestic Mt. Alberta (3619 m) in Jasper National Park was also named in her honour. When the Province of Alberta was established in 1905, the Princess expressed her gratitude by writing that she was "intensely proud of this beautiful and wonderful Province being called after me, and that my husband should have thought of it."

# Trail Blazer of the Canadian Rockies

Thomas Edmond Wilson (1859–1933) was born to Irish-Canadian parents in Bondhead, Ontario on August 21, 1859. After listening to tales of the frontier, Tom would forgo his college education and headed west. Over the next three years, his search for adventure led him to Detroit, Chicago, and Sioux City, Iowa, before returning in 1880 to join the North West Mounted Police. His first assignment was to Fort Walsh in the Cypress Hills, in southwestern Saskatchewan.

According to historian E.J. Hart "the life of police constable was rather routine, and boredom set in." After obtaining his discharge in 1881, he was hired by P.K. Hindman as a packer for Major A.B. Rogers, engineer in charge of the mountain section of the CPR main line. It was here that Wilson learned the tools of the packer's trade, mastered the famous "diamond hitch" for securing pack loads on horses and learned many skills that were key to surviving in the wilderness. His relationship with Major Rogers was often stormy, but soon both earned a grudging respect for each other and became fast friends.

Life for Wilson was not just that of a packer and trail guide; he also had a bit of the mountaineering spirit in him. He completed the first ascent of Mt. Lougheed (then Wind Mtn.) with J.J. McArthur; Storm Mtn. with W.S. Drewry; and Crowsnest Mtn. with Swiss guides hired by Edward Whymper. Wilson was also part of exploratory excursions to Mt. Assiniboine and was with the party that retrieved Philip Abbot's body from Mt. Lefroy.

Tom Wilson was part of the pioneering era that could be called "The Golden Days" of the Rocky Mountains. Not only did he have the opportunity to work with most of the historical figures of this era, he was also part of that history. In 1924, on the inaugural trip of the Trail Riders of the Canadian Rockies, a bronze plaque mounted on a large boulder containing the following inscription was unveiled on a boulder at the mouth of the Yoho Valley:

*Tom Wilson*
*Trail Blazer of*
*the Canadian Rockies*
*Lake Louise 1882*
*Emerald Lake 1882*

Tom Wilson

# Laggan

Laggan railway station ca. 1914

By the middle of October 1883, the steel rails had reached Banff and continued their persistent crawl towards the summit of the Great Divide. Only the cold weather of December forced a halt to this relentless progress just short of the summit of the Continental Divide. Near this "end of steel" a small raucous town began to grow. Some called it "Holt City" after H.S. Holt, the construction foreman of the CPR, but most knew it by another name, "The Summit." In 1884, at the suggestion of Lord Strathcona, this name was changed to Laggan after a place of the same name in Inverness, Scotland. Later, in 1886, with the renaming of Wilson's Emerald Lake to Lake Louise, Laggan officially became the hamlet of Lake Louise.

## The First Guest

Luxurious accommodation at Lake Louise has not always been the norm. The first guest of any consequence arrived by construction car in 1884. His name was A.P. Coleman, Professor of Natural History at the University of Toronto. Coleman was not impressed when he disembarked from the railroad car, describing his surroundings in the following manner: "It was evening, and my eyes turned from the mountains across the valley of Bow River to the 'city,' temporary and hideous, where night quarters must be found. The chief hotel seemed to be the 'Sumit' [Summit] House, a low-browed log building with a floor of 'puncheons' — slabs split with an axe — instead of boards." This was not a very glowing assessment of accommodation at Laggan.

Coleman's ordeal was not over for the evening and he continued by describing his first night at Summit House in a rather amusing way:

*When darkness fell I paid for my bed in advance, according to the practice of the hostelry, and retired to the grey blankets of bunk No. 2, second tier, in the common guest-chamber, trying to shut out sights and sounds from the barroom by turning my back. An hour or two later another man scrambled into the bunk, somewhat the worse for whiskey, and tucked himself into the blankets beside me. It appeared that my half-dollar paid for only half the bed.*

How times have changed!

## The First "Chalet"

With the completion of the main line in 1885, the CPR was anxious to capitalize on the beauty of the Rocky Mountains as a tourist attraction and, in accordance with the wishes of its General Manager, Cornelius Van Horne, began the construction of its mountain hotels.

Construction of the first "chalet" on the shores of Lake Louise began in 1890. It was nothing more than a crude log structure consisting of two bedrooms, a kitchen, a large sitting room, and a veranda for enjoying the scenery. William Cornelius Van Horne promoted it as "a hotel for the outdoor adventurer and alpinist." Fewer than 100 visitors were attracted to this structure in the first two years of its operation and then, in 1892, a fire destroyed the log structure.

The Chalet was rebuilt the following year with slightly larger dimensions and accommodation for up to 12 guests. By 1900 more than 5,000 tourists were being attracted yearly to the region, which necessitated expansion of the Chalet. Two "Tudor-style wings" were added that increased the capacity to 200 guests. In 1913 a concrete wing, named the Painter wing, was completed, adding

the grand Victoria Dining Room. Additional bedrooms were built in the wooden structure.

Disaster struck again on July 3, 1924, when another fire completely destroyed the wooden component of the hotel, leaving only the concrete dining room. Construction began immediately on a new eight-storey building but this time it was to be constructed from brick and concrete. The new structure was completed that same year and renamed the "Chateau Lake Louise." Except for additions in the 1990s, the main structure is essentially the same as that constructed in 1924.

**Top: The first "chalet" at Lake Louise**

**Bottom: The fire of 1924 destroys the Chalet**

# The Great Divide

Mt. Lefroy | Mt. Victoria | Mt. Collier

A splendid Rocky Mountain moment from the summit of Fairview Mtn.

Nowhere are the peaks of the Great Divide more beautiful than at Lake Louise. Their glaciated summits form the spectacular backdrop to the lake and are a constant reminder of a glaciated era long past. These mountains form the boundary between Banff and Yoho National Parks, as well as delineating the border between the provinces of Alberta and British Columbia. From their summits, waters flow east to the Atlantic Ocean via the Hudson Bay and west to the Pacific Ocean by way of the Columbia River.

Two high alpine passes, or cols, provide passageways through this seemingly insurmountable barrier: Wenkchemna Pass (2597 m) in the valley of the Ten Peaks and Abbot Pass (2926 m) between Mts. Lefroy and Victoria.

# The Story of Mt. Lefroy

James Hector named this peak in honour of Sir John Henry Lefroy (1817–1890), although there is some confusion as to which peak Hector was actually referring. During his crossing of Vermilion Pass, Hector noted, "On the opposite side of the valley I saw that the Vermilion River rises from a glacier of small size in a high valley of Mt. Lefroy."

Mt. Lefroy is not visible from Vermilion Pass, so Hector may have been referring to the small glacier on Chimney Pk. in the valley between Mt. Whymper and Boom Mtn., which is the source of the Vermilion River.

Mt. Lefroy continued to be misplaced on maps for the next 50 years. The Reverend Spotswood

Green visited the region in 1890 with the intention of climbing the peak but had to be satisfied with sketching the mountains behind Lake Louise. However, the mountain sketched by Reverend Green for his popular book *Among the Selkirk Glaciers,* and labelled Mt. Lefroy, is clearly Mt. Victoria.

The picture became even more confusing when, in 1893, Samuel Allen called what is now Mt. Lefroy, "Glacier Peak," and then, on his map of the region, misplaced not only Mt. Lefroy but also Mt. Temple. Willoughby Astley, the manager of the Chalet at Lake Louise, may have been responsible for most of this confusion because he continued to refer to the giant, helmet-shaped peak southeast of the lake as Mt. Lefroy. What he was actually pointing out to the clientele was Mt. Temple. The legend of Mt. Lefroy was just beginning.

## Mt. Lefroy 3423 m

Now that we have firmly established that Mt. Lefroy is situated in the valley of the Plain of Six Glaciers, who was this John Henry Lefroy that created all this confusion? Lefroy was an accomplished scientist noted for his studies on terrestrial magnetism. He came to Toronto in 1842 to take charge of a new observatory and remained for nine years. During 1843–44, he made an epic journey down the Mackenzie River that included a series of magnetic measurements at Fort Edmonton. Returning to England, he became scientific adviser to the War Office before he resigned from the army to become governor and commander-in-chief of the Bermudas in 1871. He was elevated to knighthood in 1832.

## The Legend Grows

Probably no other mountain in the Canadian Rockies is more responsible for attracting world attention to Lake Louise and the Canadian Alps

The "Death Trap" between Mts. Lefroy and Victoria

than Mt. Lefroy. Sadly, it would be an epic tragedy that would bring attention to these majestic peaks. However, even before that fateful day in Canadian mountaineering history, some earlier attempts on the mountain began to give Mt. Lefroy its own "mystique" of invincibility.

On July 11, 1894 three young men from Yale (Walter Wilcox, Louis Frissell, and Yandell Henderson) disembarked from the train at Laggan looking for adventure. The next day Wilcox decided to test the mettle of his companions with an attempt on Mt. Lefroy by scaling the northwest buttress from the lower Victoria Glacier. Their foolhardy attempt would almost cost Frissell his life. Was it an omen of things to come?

Wilcox had some previous climbing experience; Frissell and Henderson had none at all. Snow and ice made the conditions worse and to compound matters they only had two ice axes for the three of them. In short, they were an accident waiting to happen. The exuberance of youth and the spirit of adventure overcame what they lacked in experience, so on July 12, 1894 they started up the lower Victoria Glacier. Crossing without incident, they began ascending a coulier to a chimney in the north buttress of Mt. Lefroy. They abandoned the snow in favour of rock ledges and scrambled to a

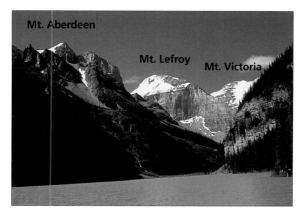

Mt. Aberdeen

Mt. Lefroy

Mt. Victoria

Panoramic view
across Lake Louise

Sir John Henry Lefroy,
Founder of Canadian Meteorology

position approximately 200 m above the glacier. Henderson described the disaster that befell the party:

*Wilcox climbed up and warned me, as I followed, not to touch a loose rock some three feet long and two feet thick — we met it again at the foot of the cliff and I measured it ... When I had reached a point about eight feet from the boulder, and where the ledge was only about two feet wide, and was starting to climb to the next ledge, I heard something slipping and looking around saw Frissell and the boulder sliding off the ledge together.*

Henderson quickly took up slack on the rope and then braced himself for the jolt that was to come:

*Then the jerk came as Frissell struck on the lower ledge with a good part of his six feet two inches well over the edge ... Although I took no notice of it at the time, as I had much else to think of, I found next day that, owing to the way I caught the rope in my haste, the jerk had burnt the skin from inside of the first two fingers and the back of the third and little finger of my right hand.*

Miraculously, Frissell's fall had been stopped but he was laying precariously on a small ledge, bleeding from a head wound and knocked unconscious for an instant. Applying snow to the wound quickly stopped the bleeding and brought Frissell to his senses. Frissell "urged us to leave him and go up the mountain, but of course we refused and in the course of half an hour we were able to lift him to his feet, although in spite of every effort he was unable to walk." Somehow with great effort and leadership on the part of Wilcox, they lowered Frissell down a few ledges by "sliding around the schrunds until we reached the foot of the coulier. There we placed Frissell on a little pile of rock ..." from where Wilcox scurried over the glacier back to the Chalet at Lake Louise for help.

Henderson and Frissell huddled together on the glacier and awaited the arrival of help from the Chalet. At 6:00 p.m. help arrived and using a litter, quickly constructed from two poles and a piece of canvas, the rescue party slid Frissell off the glacier. Frissell quickly recovered from his wounds to join Allen and Wilcox on

Philip Stanley Abbot

Perhaps Thompson expressed it best, when from the summit of Mt. Fairview he stated, "our greedy hearts were filled with a desire for its topmost bit of crystal, rock or ice." Abbot came back with Fay and Thompson in the summer of 1896, but this time they had added Professor George Little, a competent climber, to the team. Cautiously they ascended the Death Trap, fully conscious of every cracking sound coming from the overhanging glacier above their heads. It was with great relief that they reached the high col at 11:50 a.m. Professor Charles Fay best described the rest of the events of that historic day in a stirring memorial to Philip Abbot written for the journal Appalachia adapted as follows.

From the col the summit was within reach. Abbot was exhilarated, joyfully exclaiming, "The peak is ours!" And surely it would be, for after surveying the route ahead his heart began to pound with excitement and his "enthusiasm found ample expression in that ever happy smile, his beaming eyes, and his quiet remark — and what was ever so convincing as that confident, almost childlike mental repose?" Time became timeless and their step cutting endless as they zigzagged up the ice-slopes. At 5:30 p.m. they had reached the crux, "an immense bastion possibly seventy-five feet in height, behind which lay the summit, of which as yet, owing to foreshortening, we had no satisfactory view."

What happened next nobody knows for sure. Abbot informed the climbers that he had found a route through a vertical cleft to the summit and Fay continued:

*Bidding Thompson and me to unrope and keep under cover from falling stones, he clambered some thirty feet up the rift, secured a good anchorage,*

the first ascent of Mt. Temple a few days later. The legend of Mt. Lefroy continued to grow.

The next year, 1895, Philip S. Abbot, Charles Fay, and Charles S. Thompson attempted to climb the mountain, not once but twice. Both times they were repelled. Fay described their attempt after reaching the base of the Death Trap: "By this time it had begun to rain and miniature cascades were soon drenching us from the overhanging upper edge of our chimney. Evidently the Fates were against us, and we withdrew, with a feeling that Lefroy was our debtor." Thompson added his feelings, and wrote, "I have taken baths of ice-cold Lake Michigan water with set tooth and undismayed determination; but the chill of that falling torrent was beyond endurance." Below him Fay enjoyed every moment "with fiendish delight." Rebuffed, they vowed to return the next year.

## Tragedy!

Abbot became obsessed with conquering the mountain, dreaming and planning its demise day and night during the winter of 1895–96.

Abbot's search party; from left to right, Tom Wilson, George T. Little, H. Ashley, and Charles Fay

*and called upon Professor Little to follow. This the latter proceeded to do, but while standing at the bottom of the cleft preparing to climb, he received a tingling blow from a small stone dislodged by the rope. A moment later a larger one falling upon the rope half severed it, so as to require a knot. As danger from this source seemed likely to continue, our leader had Little also free himself from the rope and come up to where he stood. From here a shelf led around to the left, along which Abbot now proceeded a few yards and discovered a gully leading upward, unseen from the point first attained, and this also he began to ascend. To Mr. Little's question, whether it might not be better to try and turn the bastion on the shelf itself, he replied: "I think not. I have a good lead here."*

These were the last words Phillip Abbot ever uttered. "A moment later, Little, whose attention was for the moment diverted to another portion of the crag, was conscious that

something had fallen swiftly past him and knew only too well what it must be." Abbot rolled down the slope, the rope coiling around him, until his limp body came to rest on a narrow plateau some 900 ft. below. It took three hours for the rest of the party to reach the plateau and:

*To our surprise life was not yet extinct. The fatal wound in the back of the head, evidently received in the short initial fall of perhaps twenty feet, was the only grievous outward mark, and the autopsy proved that not a limb was broken. A faint murmur that my imagination interpreted as a recognition of our presence and an expression of gratitude that we had a least escaped from peril, alone broke the silence for a brief moment, and then we three bared our heads in the twilight, believing that his generous spirit was already passing.*

Miraculously, Abbot began to breathe again!

*With tender hands, having first disentangled the ropes, we*

*raised him, and began the dreary descent; but we had scarcely reached the brink of the little cliff when he again ceased to breath. Not satisfied with this evidence, we tested pulse and heart. That all was over in the mortal life of our beloved companion was subject to no manner of doubt.*

Macabre as it may seem, this accident on Mt. Lefroy put the Canadian Rockies on the world's mountaineering stage.

## Triumph!

Mt. Lefroy had to be conquered if only to commemorate the spirit of a gallant Philip Abbot. To this end Professor Charles Fay planned the next year's ascent down to the last detail. He invited the best climbers of the day to join the 1897 expedition and, most importantly, obtained the services of renowned professional Swiss guide Peter Sarbach to lead the party.

They crossed Lake Louise in a rowboat at 2:40 a.m. on August 2, 1897, and five hours later they were at the summit of Abbot Pass. Sarbach then roped the party into three

groups and, without incident, successfully guided the climbers up the same slopes that had produced disaster just the year previous. On the summit they celebrated their achievement by building a cairn to the memory of Abbot's spirit.

## Abbot Pass 2925 m

In 1893 Samuel Allen and Walter Wilcox made two unsuccessful attempts to reach the summit of Mt. Victoria (then Mt. Green). The first attempt was abruptly halted by the presence of a maze of concealed crevasses on the lower Victoria Glacier. The second attempt skirted the bases of what are now Popes Pk. and Mt. Collier, but it too ended in failure. It was during this second attempt that they made a momentous discovery as they witnessed avalanches thundering off the upper Victoria Glacier into the narrow defile between Mts. Lefroy and Victoria. Allen sat in awe and gave this description:

*Across the narrow valley was Mount Lefroy, its west arête seen almost in profile. I noticed a coulier reaching from the glacier below almost to the*

Members of the Mt. Lefroy first ascent party including Professor Charles Fay (seated front left) and Swiss guide Peter Sarbach (seated front right)

**Left: Abbot Hut**

**Right: Lake Oesa from Abbot Pass**

*snow plateau above the west buttress, and thought then, as now, that early in the season the plateau could be reached, whence the arête is apparently not difficult. I was constrained, from the frequency with which avalanches fell into it from the crest, to call the narrow valley S. of Mount Lefroy, and the col connecting it with the crest, by the name of "Death Trap."*

Little did Allen or Wilcox realize at the time how prophetic that name would become.

Allen believed another, much safer route to the summit of the Death Trap existed and he was determined to find it. In the summer of 1894, Allen returned with Stoney friend, Yule Carryer, to Lake O'Hara in the hope of finding such a route. Here they discovered Lake Oesa, "a placid lake, a dark blue circle about 1/2 mile in diameter. The glaciers clustered around its farther end, whence floating blocks of ice dotted with white the sapphire surface,

while behind and above rose the slopes of a grand amphitheatre ... "

Allen had discovered his route to the top of the Death Trap.

Allen began to ascend the gorge in that grand amphitheatre: "A foothold, a couple of handholds, a wriggle, a moment of doubt, and I lay poised upon a fine ledge, whence ascent to the col was less difficult. Carryer had found easier work on the right side, and was awaiting me on the summit. We were standing on top of the 'Death Trap.'"

In *The Alpine Journal*, Allen writes that, "a proposition has been made, in which I heartily concur, to name this pass in memory of Mr. Philip Stanley Abbot, who, in the past summer, in an ascent straight up from the col, lost his life through an accident when the summit of Mount Lefroy was almost within his grasp."

## The Hut in the Clouds

In 1921 renowned Swiss guide Edward Feuz Jr. suggested that a stone shelter be built at Abbot Pass. The following summer Swiss guides hauled two tons of supplies up to this high col through the Death Trap. Everything from materials for constructing the building to household furnishings had to be ferried to the pass, first by pack horses as far as crevasses on the glacier would allow, and then on the backs of the guides.

The shelter they built was at a higher altitude than any other building in Canada at that time and could comfortably accommodate 24 people. At the official ceremonial opening, Edward Feuz Jr. said, "Down in the valley, a house, a big house, is just a house. But up here, in the ice and snow, with all those beautiful peaks everywhere, this simple hut is home." It too was named in honour of Abbot and remained the the highest altitude structure in Canada until 1982 when it was surpassed (by a mere 15 m) with the construction of the Neil Colgan Hut above Moraine Lake.

# Homage to a Queen

## Mt. Victoria 3464 m

Mt. Victoria is the spectacular mountain that forms the backdrop for Lake Louise. It just may be the most photographed mountain in the entire Rocky Mountains. A long snow-covered ridge separates the higher South Pk. (3464 m) from the lower North Pk. (3388 m) located just west of Mt. Collier. The peak was known by various names before J.J. McArthur officially bestowed the name "Victoria" in 1886 to honour Queen Victoria (1819–1901) in the jubilee year of her reign. Prior to that, the Reverend Spotswood Green (1847–1919) mistakenly referred to the mountain as Mt. Lefroy when he

Mt. Victoria — the mountain that had to be named after a queen!

Left: Queen Victoria

Right: Avalanche on
Mt. Victoria

visited Lake Louise in 1889 and
Samuel Allen named the peak
Mt. Green in his honour.

In August 1897, two days after the
fall on Mt. Lefroy, J. Norman Collie,
Charles Fay, Arthur Michael, and
guide Peter Sarbach made the first
ascent of the South Pk. of Mt.
Victoria. The first ascent of this majestic peak caused Charles Fay to
contemplate his mortality. In a remarkable passage from *Appalachia,*
he wrote:

> ... the sky began to grow paler
> about the brilliant morning
> star, and this pallor, caught by
> the lofty snows on Lefroy and
> Victoria, brought out their vast
> hovering forms like weird and
> portentous spectres. There was
> something uncanny in the

> spectacle, something to raise
> the question whether our at-
> tempt was not sacrilege, and
> whether it was not the match-
> ing of impotent mortal powers
> against the forces supernatural
> and remorseless.

# A Tragic Day on Victoria

A small jovial party of Mexican women from the Alpine Club of Mexico arrived in Banff on July 27, 1954, intent on climbing Mt. Lefroy, Mt. Victoria, and Castle Mtn. The exuberant group of seven was led by their interpreter Ofeliz Fernandez and their Mexican guide Eduardo Sanvicente. Sanvicente was not without highly rated qualifications, having scaled the Matterhorn; Mt. McKinley; and Mt. Aconcagua in Argentina, the highest peak in the western hemisphere. After arriving at Lake Louise Sanvicente consulted with veteran Swiss guide Walter Feuz about their intended ascents and was advised by Feuz against trying Mts. Victoria or Lefroy with only one guide. Sanvicente disregarded Feuz's advice — perhaps because all the Mexican women were considered to be experienced mountain climbers or perhaps because of his belief in his own skills. On September 28, the party hiked to the Tea House at the Plain of Six Glaciers where they camped for the night and anxiously waited for morning.

Early the next morning they proceeded through the Death Trap and reached Abbot Pass without incident. By all accounts they spent a pleasant evening in Abbot Hut preparing for an ascent of Mt. Victoria the next day. Excitement and anticipation were running high that morning of July 30 as the seven climbers formed two ropes. The lead four-person rope consisting of Maria Louis Fabila, Beatriz Diaz, and Lucia Ocaranza was anchored by Eduardo, while rope number two consisted of Ofelia Fernandez, Carmen Rubio, and Maria Garcia. Only Marguerita Vivenco was left at the hut; she was to prepare food upon their triumphant return.

Swiss guide Peter Sarbach had es-

The jubilant Mexican summit party before the tragedy

tablished the rock ridge route to the 3464 m summit in 1897 and the route was considered quite safe. However, Sanvicente chose to ascend the steep, previously unscaled eastern snow face! This face reaches, in places, inclines of 50 to 60°, which the party easily scaled with the aid of their crampons. Shortly after noon, the triumphant party reached the south summit. This was the first ever ascent via the eastern snow face. For some inexplicable reason, instead of descending the normal rock ridge route they chose to descend the steep snow face again! Eminent Swiss guides Walter and Ernest Feuz were intermittently following their progress through binoculars below at Lake Louise and Ernest said simply, "I knew if they didn't fall, they would have been darn lucky."

Snow conditions had drastically changed since their ascent. The heat of the afternoon sun had softened the surface considerably, while the snow beneath remained firm presenting the climbers with a dangerous situation. Aware that the snow could break loose at any moment, the party moved gingerly. Again, Walter Feuz noted from far below that the climbers had made a serious blunder; instead of descending one at a time, leaving others to anchor

**101**

the lead in case of a fall, they were all moving at the same time. Not only that, they had failed to remove their crampons, which while excellent on ice, are useless and even dangerous on soft snow.

A tragedy was in the making and scarcely 100 m below the summit it happened. Ofelia Fernandez, on the second rope, described in horror the events that followed: "I saw position three start to slip and drag the others down. They slid down and then they all tangled up in a ball and rolled down very fast. There was no avalanche. When I saw them fall, I knew it was all over." Horror-stricken, the three women on the second rope saw their comrades and guide tumble down the face, bounce over a rock ridge into space and then over a cliff into the Death Trap almost 200 m below. Stunned by what had happened and unable to move for fear of suffering the same fate, the three remaining climbers huddled together on the steep face praying to be rescued.

Walter Feuz again trained his binoculars on the snow face but this time, finding only three climbers, realized a tragedy had occurred. He notified Lake Louise Chateau manager E.C. Pitt and quickly formed a rescue party. They were in a race against time to reach the stranded women before they inadvertently tried something foolish and also plunged to their deaths. Ernest Feuz headed the party, which consisted of Charles Rowland, Ray Wehner, and Frank Campbell (medical students working as bellboys at the Chateau and part-time climbers) and Harry Green, a member of the Alpine Club. The rescue party reached the Tea House at 4:40 p.m.

Quickly they ascended the Death Trap and scarcely paused as they passed the bodies of the victims. One quick glance told them all they needed to know. Their objective was to save the three climbers huddled above. Racing on, they reached the pass where they were greeted by Marguerita, who was trying desperately to light a fire in order to prepare a meal for her comrades, and completely unaware that tragedy had befallen her friends.

Only Ernest Feuz and Rowland set off from the hut and raced up the rock ridge at a pace that astonished the young Rowland, given the fact that Ernest was 65 years old! In 35 minutes they reached a saddle on the ridge directly above the stranded climbers. They secured a firm belay and tied two ropes together from which Rowland descended the snow slope, cutting steps as he went. Securely belayed by Feuz from above, the three frightened women were eventually pulled to the safety off the ridge. Feuz immediately removed their crampons and they began a slow, cautious two-hour descent to the safety and warmth of Abbot Hut.

Feuz wanted to avoid even more trauma to the women and decided to get the four survivors past the bodies in darkness even though they only possessed flashlights and one climbing lantern. They left the pass at 10:30 p.m. in total darkness and when they came to the spot where their four comrades lay the lights were intentionally aimed in such a way that they were able to pass within 5 m of the victims without the four survivors even being aware of the presence of their bodies. They reached the safety of the Tea House at 1:30 a.m.

One of the most incredible mountain rescues in the history of the Canadian Alps was finally over. Ernest Feuz and Charles Rowland had displayed almost superhuman strength in climbing to the top of Mt. Victoria, plucking three frightened women from a dangerous snow slope, leading them down the rock ridge to Abbot Pass, and guiding them down the Death Trap to the Tea House on the Plain of Six Glaciers in only nine hours.

# Hidden from View

Mt. Collier   Pope's Pk.   Mt. Whyte   Mt. Niblock

## Mt. Collier 3215 m

Mt. Collier is located between the North Pk. of Mt. Victoria and Popes Pk. immediately to the north. Samuel Allen had originally named the peak Mt. Nichols in honour of his climbing companion on Mt. Fox during the summer of 1893, the Reverend H.P. Nichols of Minneapolis. In 1903 the mountain was officially named after Joseph Collier M.D., a British physician, who, with his brother Gordon and guide Christian Kaufman, made the first ascent of the mountain that same year.

## Popes Pk. 3126 m

This stunning peak is best viewed from either the Icefields Parkway or from the Trans-Canada Highway just east of Wapta Lake. Only then does this mountain reveal its striking, glacial-capped summit. Samuel Allen originally named this peak Mt. D'Espine, after his friend and climbing companion on the Matterhorn, M.E. d'Espine of Geneva, Switzerland. Later it became known as Boundary Pk. because it was located on the boundary of the original Rocky Mountains National Park. Officially it was named Popes Pk. in honour of long-time Canadian politician John Henry Pope.

John Henry Pope (1824–1889) was born in Eaton Township in Lower Canada and received his education at Compton High School. As a member of the Conservative Party, he ran for office, but was defeated three times before being acclaimed as a member of parliament in 1857. He represented the riding of Compton in the House of Commons until his death in 1889.

Originally a farmer, Pope was one of the first Canadians to attempt improving cattle herds by importing thoroughbred stock. With this background he was appointed Minister of Agriculture in 1871 and became the first minister to focus on agricultural issues facing Canada. During his second term in office, Pope also became Acting Minister of Railways and Canals and became involved in

Peaks on the skyline from the summit of Fairview Mtn.

Mt. Niblock  Mt. Whyte  Pope's Pk.  Mt. Victoria

The magnificent north face of Popes Pk. viewed from the Icefields Parkway

the procurement of controversial funds and loans that ensured final construction of the railway by the CPR. Pope officially became Minister of Railways and Canals in 1885, a post he held until his death from liver cancer in 1889.

John Henry Pope

# Lake Agnes

Larch season at Lake Agnes

*Lake Agnes is a wild tarn imprisoned by cheerless cliffs. At one end there is a narrow fringe of trees, but the lake on either side is bordered by barren angular stones, where nothing grows. Its northward exposure and the towering walls of a great amphitheatre keep out the sun and allow the snow to linger here all summer.*
Walter Wilcox, 1896

## Who Was Agnes?

The same year that Tom Wilson discovered Lake Louise, Edwin Hunter informed him of two other small alpine tarns generally referred to as the "Lakes in the Clouds" because they were located high above the "Lake of Little Fishes." One of these small tarns was referred to as the "Goat's Looking Glass" because, according to an ancient legend, this was "where the goats came down to

Fairview Mtn.

Mt. Temple

it to use as a mirror while they combed their beards." Today this tiny tarn is officially called Mirror Lake.

The origin of the name for the upper tarn (2118 m), named Lake Agnes, is somewhat confusing. In 1886 Willoughby Astley, the first manager of the Chalet at Lake Louise, escorted an Agnes Knox from Toronto to the Lakes in the Clouds. She was the first woman to visit the lake. Was it named in her honour?

A few days later, Astley received notice that Lady Macdonald, wife of the first Prime Minister of Canada, was to visit Lake Louise. Astley escorted Lady Macdonald, a

**Lady Agnes Macdonald**

Mrs. Scarth from Winnipeg, and NWMP Captain Harper of Banff, to the same lake. Lady Macdonald was led to believe that she was the first woman to visit the lake and that it would be named in her honour. The CPR had a predicament on its hands. Whose name would be given to the lake? As fate would have it, Lady Macdonald's middle name happened to be Agnes and all agreed to name it Lake Agnes. Does it really matter which Agnes the lake is named after? A visit to Lake Agnes in the fall when the larches have turned colour is a scene never to be forgotten.

A spectacular view of Lake Louise and Lake Agnes (bottom right) from the summit of Mt. St. Piran

# Above Lake Agnes

Mt. Whyte     Mt. Niblock     Mt. St. Piran     Little Beehive     Big Beehive

*Panorama of peaks from Lake Louise*

## Devil's Thumb
## 2458 m

In August 1891 Samuel Allen was returning home to Philadelphia from an excursion to the Sierras in California and climbing in the Selkirk Mtns. when he stopped for a brief visit at Lake Louise. He closed his season with a hike to Lake Agnes where he "noticed at the left extremity of the latter a towering aiguille, absolutely vertical from the lake."

Allen described his ascent:

*In the hope of turning it in flank or rear I ascended the ledge of that peculiar mountain locally known as the "Beehive" to the top of the latter, whence I was able, by following the narrower ledges, to turn a corner and reach a wider gorge, choked by a vast boulder, upon which the remainder of its accompanying avalanche had come to rest. I could reach a portion of it, but, not knowing*

*how securely it was wedged, hesitated to experiment with it. I finally passed the place and made the pinnacle.*

Allen had just completed the first ascent of this needle-like edifice and the view from the top whetted his appetite. It was from here that he viewed, for the first time, "the summit neve of Mount Temple," the mountain with which he would become "obsessed."

## Mt. St. Piran
## 2649 m

Samuel Allen named this peak Mt. Piran after a town near Ligger Bay on the north shore of Cornwall, the birthplace of Willoughby John Astley (1859–1948), the first manager of the Chalet at Lake Louise. "St." was later added to to the name of the mountain. Astley ran sternwheelers for the CPR on the Arrow Lakes in British Columbia and performed a similar service for the British army on the

Mt. Whyte

Mt. Niblock

Devil's Thumb

Mt. Whyte

Nile River during WWI. Walter Wilcox named Lake Annette in Paradise Valley in honour of Astley's wife.

## Mt. Niblock 2976 m

John Niblock (1849–1914), of Irish ancestry, was superintendent of the Western Division of the CPR for several years at the turn of the century. I guess it was nice to be an official of the CPR in the early days as it ensured a rocky monument would be named after you. In 1899 Walter D. Wilcox completed the first ascent, a solo effort from Lake Agnes.

## Mt. Whyte 2983 m

Walter Wilcox named this peak in 1898 for Sir William Whyte (1843–1914), who was employed by the CPR in 1884 as superintendent of its Ontario Division. Later he became the second Vice-President of the Western Division of the CPR. In 1901 three of the Swiss guides employed by Edward Whymper (C. Kaufmann, C. Klucker, and J. Pollinger) completed the first ascent of the peak from Lake Agnes.

Top: Panorama from the summit of Mt. St. Piran

Bottom left: Lake Agnes teahouse

Bottom right: John Niblock and companion at Laggan

# Georgia Engelhard Cromwell: Best of Her Time

Ernest Feuz and Georgia Engelhard on Mt. Victoria

Edward Feuz Jr. recounted that "three women mountaineers of my time were way above the rest. One was an American, another an English lady [Katie Gardiner], and the third, by far the best, was a native Canadian [Phyllis Munday]. The American was Georgia Engelhard. She was tough and wiry and climbed so fast she often had us guides puffing to keep up." Georgia had to overcome her personal fear of heights to become one of the most prominent female mountaineers in Canada and one that left her own personal legacy on the Lake Louise region.

Georgia was born on November 19, 1906, in New York City, to wealthy and sophisticated parents who introduced her to hiking and photography. A "spirited" child she attended an exclusive private school and became a proficient painter.

At first, Georgia was not particularly attracted to mountaineering. In writings recorded in *Lake Louise: A Diamond in the Wilderness,* she stated, "I first came to the Chateau Lake Louise in 1926 with my parents. In my teens I had visited the Alps and the Dolomites and thought them handsome but to me mountain climbing was just an insane sport." All changed in 1926 during a family trip to Mt. Rainier Park in Washington where, initiated to the sport, she "became crazy for it."

Lake Louise became the ideal centre for her mountaineering escapades. It was here that she met Edward Feuz Jr. who guided her to the summit of Pinnacle Mtn. (3067 m) in just three hours. Edward said, "Waal, she just stuck her head in my rucksack and so I ran." She was only 20 years old and she was hooked! At the tender age of 22, Georgia became the youngest female member of the American Alpine Club.

It wasn't long before her speed on the trail and in climbing a mountain approached legendary status. Just after Georgia had hired Edward Feuz Jr. to guide her up one of Mt. Murchison's towers, his brother Ernest warned him, "You've got a fine lady, but watch out. When she starts uphill, she goes like a rocket. What she needs is a mountain goat, not a guide." Some of the guides even contemplated filling her rucksack with a "few rocks" in order to slow her down!

Soon her determination, strength and endurance became the stuff of legend. During an outing at Lake Louise in 1929 she accomplished quite a feat, and recounted, "In nine days I climbed nine peaks: Lefroy, the traverse of the two Pope's Peaks, the traverse of Haddo and Aberdeen, Hungabee, Huber, Victoria and Biddle." And then on the day of her departure she arose at 4:00 a.m. and scrambled to the summit of Mt. St. Piran before catching the train. In 1931, during one period in the Selkirk Mts., she made 32 ascents, 24 of them in three weeks!

To say she loved Lake Louise would be an understatement. She climbed Mt. Victoria 13 times, including the time in 1933 with Ernest Feuz Jr. when they made the first "impossible" south-to-north traverse of the mountain. In 1935, while in Europe, she met her future husband Tony Cromwell and together they completed over 60 ascents. She amassed a record of ascents in the Canadian Rockies that is unmatched by any other woman and very few men.

Georgia wrote, "Probably the best compliment I received was from Ernest after Tony and I had done the Victoria, Collier, Pope's Peaks traverse. He shook his head sadly and muttered: 'Dat Chorcha, she vants to do too much.' " Legendary guide Edward Feuz Jr. considered Georgia to be "by far the best" female mountaineer of her times.

# The Slate Range

This is a minor range of peaks north of the Bow River across from the town of Lake Louise. In the valley most of the peaks in this range are hidden from view by Mt. Whitehorn, but they form a spectacular skyline when viewed from higher elevations to be had on the access roads to Lake Louise and Moraine Lake. James Hector was responsible for naming the range when he journeyed up the Pipestone River on his second visit to the region in 1859.

## Mt. Whitehorn
## 2630 m

The origin of the name is uncertain. Apparently this minor peak, when covered in snow, resembled a huge white horn to someone interested in naming a mountain. It is most famous for its ski runs, annually hosting a World Cup event on its slopes.

## Lipalian Mtn.
## 2728 m

Lipalian is a geological term that attempts to explain the sudden

Mt. Whitehorn    Redoubt Mtn.    Lipalian Mtn.

Top: Some peaks of the Slate Range from Moraine Lake Road

Bottom: An early snowfall on Redoubt Mtn.

appearance of abundant life between the apparent "lifeless" Precambrian time period (800 million years ago) and the Cambrian period (550 million years ago). Unlike Precambrian indications of life, Cambrian life forms are comparatively highly developed and diverse. Lipalian Mtn. was named after this "gap" in knowledge because it is composed of the youngest Precambrian rocks in North America.

## Redoubt Mtn. 2902 m

Military fortifications and camps were often protected by an impregnable defensive structure constructed around an enclosure termed a "redoubt." No doubt the formidable rock formations resembling a huge military redoubt were responsible for A.O. Wheeler's name for this mountain.

## Mt. Richardson 3086 m

This, the highest peak of the Slate Range, was named by James Hector in honour of Dr. John Richardson (1787–1865), a surgeon and naturalist who worked on two of Franklin's expeditions to the Arctic. Richardson was not present on the ill-fated expedition of 1845 when all members perished due to cold, hunger, and lead poisoning, but he did aid Dr. John Rae in his search for Franklin.

## Merlin Castle 2840 m

Evidently an early visitor to the region, in a state of euphoria or altered consciousness, thought that the impressive towers or pinnacles of this peak reminded the traveller of the magician Merlin's abode during King Arthur's time.

## Pika Pk. 3023 m

This is one of the few peaks in the Rockies named after tiny inhabitants of rockslides and boulder fields in the montane and alpine zones.

Merlin Castle | Mt. Richardson | Pika Pk. | Ptarmigan Pk.

Pikas, *Ochotona princeps,* are small mammals that belong to the Order Lagomorpha, which also includes rabbits and hares. This order has two sets of incisors, which distinguishes it from rodents. For this reason they are often called "rock rabbits." Every hiker in the high country has heard their high-pitched "bleating" as they announce the presence of unwanted strangers into their territory.

## Ptarmigan Pk.
## 3059 m

J.W.A. Hickson named this peak after a flock of white-tailed ptarmigan he sighted on the peak during his first ascent with Edward Feuz Jr. in 1909. The white-tailed ptarmigan, *Lagopus leucurus,* is a permanent mountain resident that inhabits moist meadows along alpine streams. *Lagopus* is Latin for "foot of the rabbit," which refers to its heavily feathered legs that help create a "snowshoe" effect for easier locomotion on the alpine snow pack. Another distinctive trait of the white-tailed ptarmigan is its change of plumage with the seasons. In the spring and summer the species assumes a mottled brown-grey colouration; in the winter it is completely white except for its beak, eyes, and claws.

Top: More peaks of the Slate Range from the Little Beehive

Bottom left: White-tailed ptarmigan

Bottom right: Pika

# Paradise Valley

## Discovery

Mt. Temple

Paradise Valley and Creek from the summit of Fairview Mtn.

Prior to 1894 very little was known of the mountains east of Lake Louise. On July 30, 1894, Walter Wilcox, Samuel Allen, Yandell Henderson, and George Warrington set out from Lake Louise to explore the valley between Mts. Lefroy and Aberdeen. Their discovery of Paradise Valley was totally by accident. Wilcox recounted: "In fact, we were making an expedition for the purpose of finding a practicable route up Hazel Peak [Mt. Aberdeen]." On a "cloudy cheerless" day they rowed across Lake Louise, roped and began ascending the Victoria Glacier to its junction with the Lefroy Glacier, which descended from the slopes of a peak they christened the "Mitre" due to its resemblance to the shape of a bishop's cap. The region between the two peaks was a dreadful place of ice and perpetual snow, devoid of any vegetation. Combined with the sombre conditions of the day, Wilcox described their surroundings as "a magnificent canyon of desolate grandeur."

"Proceeding cautiously, as we approached the very summit, to avoid the danger of an overhanging cornice of snow, we had no sooner arrived on the highest part than we beheld a valley of surpassing beauty, wide and beautiful, with alternating open meadows and rich forests." Walter Wilcox could hardly suppress his amazement at the scene before him as the "Yale Club" attained the summit of Mitre Pass. Wilcox continued, "This beautiful scene, which has taken some time to describe, even superficially, burst on our view

Mt. Lefroy

Mt. Aberdeen

The Mitre

so suddenly that for a time the cliffs echoed to exclamations of and shouts, while those who had recently been most depressed in spirit were now most vehement in expressions of delight." Samuel Allen christened the valley using the Stoney term Wastach, meaning "beautiful," but Wilcox insisted on calling it Paradise Valley.

The others were equally impressed. Allen wrote, "As we stepped upon the narrow ridge, 9,000 feet above the sea, the view beyond was indeed beautiful, which, by the Indian equivalent, Wastach [Stoney for beautiful or wonderful], I entitled it." Henderson also treasured this moment and said, "As we were the first to surmount this pass and to see this valley we built a cairn and named our valley Paradise Valley."

Mt. Hungabee

Ringrose Pk.

Top: High col between Mt. Aberdeen (left) and the Mitre (centre) from which the Yale Club discovered Paradise Valley.

Bottom: Upper reaches of Paradise Valley and Horseshoe Glacier from Mt. Temple

# The Giant Steps and Horseshoe Glacier

The G ant Steps

joked that it had been quite an eventful day for Warrington, first falling into a crevasse and now this happening, on his first experience in the mountains.

Rushing down to the warmth and pleasant surroundings of the valley bottom, Allen said they discovered that the stream "flowed from the west end of a magnificent semi-circular glacier which I called the Half-moon Glacier." Wilcox preferred the name Horseshoe Glacier and that is its official name today. At the head of the valley they discovered meltwater from this glacier cascaded in "leaps and falls over immense rectangular blocks of stone, and a succession of truly remarkable views are to be obtained from the banks as the water descends these giant steps of solid rock." These are the Giant Steps.

An insurmountable wall of rock (made up of Wenkchemna Pk., Mt. Hungabee, Ringrose Pk., Glacier Pk., and Mt. Lefroy) guards the head of Paradise Valley. Horseshoe Glacier encircles their feet. Allen commented on this scene while descending from Mt. Temple:

*Below us, lies the broad valley which I have designated Wastach, or Beautiful; its southern end bounded by the watershed, consisting here of the magnificent rock-peaks Mts. Hungabee and Ringrose, whose feet are encircled by a curving glacier, a crescent of sapphire blue, from either tip of which flow streams to form the Wastach River [Paradise Creek].*

## Mt. Hungabee 3492 m

One peak dominates the wall of mountains at the head of Paradise Valley. Seeming to rise out of Horse-

A fter spending half an hour at the Mitre col taking pictures, surveying the new landscape, and building a "stone man" to commemorate their ascent, the four adventurers made a unanimous decision to turn their backs on the cold and desolate ascent route and descend into Paradise Valley. Once again their inexperience surfaced as they began to glissade down a snow slope into the valley. As fate would have it, Warrington would again wear the horns of the scapegoat as he fell and initiated an uncontrolled tumble by the group down the snow-covered slope. Somehow they managed to arrest their slide and emerged in a gigantic heap of twisted rope and bodies that Wilcox likened to being "enmeshed like flies in a spider's web." They could only laugh at their predicament and

shoe Glacier is a magnificent peak with a double summit that Allen saw fit to name Hungabee, the Stoney word for "Chieftain." It is sometimes referred to as the "savage peak."

On August 3, 1903, Herschell C. Parker and guides Christian and Hans Kaufmann decided to attempt Mt. Hungabee from Prospector's Valley. It became a breathtaking effort, which included an exciting airy traverse over a tremendously steep snow slope that fell thousands of feet into Paradise Valley. That wasn't even the crux, which came when they were confronted with a narrow "gable," or break in the arête, a short distance from the summit. The narrowness of the arête prevented simply jumping across this break. Parker described the sensational manner in which this crux was overcome:

*… slowly and carefully, while firmly grasping the rock on one side, Christian thrust his feet forward until they touched the other and his body bridged the chasm; then a strong forward swing, and he stood safely beyond the gap. For me, aided by the rope, the matter was far less difficult and soon we made our*

*way over the intervening arête, gained the corniced summit, and Hungabee, the grim old "Chieftain," at last was conquered.*

Mt. Hungabee and Ringrose Pk. at the head of Paradise Valley from Coral Creek picnic area on the Bow Valley Parkway

## Ringrose Pk. 3281 m

Samuel Allen named this peak after a "Mr. A.E.L. Ringrose, of London, an extensive traveller, and of great familiarity with the Rockies," during his historic single-day effort from Paradise valley to Opabin Pass. Neither Mt. Hungabee nor Ringrose Pk. is readily visible to most visitors without hiking up Paradise Valley, however a glimpse of these two peaks can be obtained from the Coral Creek picnic area on the Bow Valley Parkway a few kilometres east of Lake Louise.

# Mountains, Men, and Monuments

First came the mountains, uplifted on the back of the Pacific Plate in a monumental collision with the North American Plate some 100 million years ago. Much later they were invaded by masses of ice that ripped away at their faces and carved spectacular edifices. They were monuments to nature. And then came man. He was overcome by their power. Mountain landscapes are the most powerful in the world and man began to worship these cathedrals. Mountains came to be the sacred home of myths and legends of the supernatural. Some men feared the mountains; others attempted to capture their grandeur on canvas. Still others could not resist raising their eyes to the sky, contemplating their heights. Suddenly they became summits to conquer. Only then did they become monuments to man festooned with names he attached to their peaks. Who were these mortals?

# The Yale Lake Louise Club

Once the CPR had pushed its main line from Banff to Laggan the mountains were about to experience a new type of adventurer, one not just satisfied with exploring the mountain wilderness but intent on climbing these peaks.

In 1891, Samuel Allen a young freshman from Yale arrived at Lake Louise and experienced a "Rocky Mountain High." His stay was brief but he would return with an exuberant group of young classmates from Yale: Walter D. Wilcox, Yandell Henderson, Lewis Frissell, and George Warrington. Together they would explore new valleys, climb untrodden peaks, and become responsible for most of the beautiful names we associate with the landmarks in this region.

By today's mountaineering standards, they were totally inexperienced. Henderson, by his own admission, recollected:

> As regards mountaineering, Wilcox and Allen may each have made one or two conventional ascents with guides in Switzerland — I do not now remember. For the rest of us the pages of the Badminton volume on 'Mountaineering,' read after we reached Lake Louise, were our only source of information. We read up the night before and next morning applied our information in practice on mountains that are in some respects the most dangerous in the world. We had hobnailed boots, ropes and ice-axes. We had also that spirit of adventure that gets boys into tight places and (generally) gets them out again.

What this new breed lacked in mountaineering skills they made up for with the exuberance of youth, lack of fear from hazards of the unknown, and the desire for adventure.

## Samuel Evans Stokes Allen (1874–1945)

Samuel E.S. Allen (photo, page 137) made only four visits to the Rockies but he would leave a legacy perhaps unmatched in the annals of exploratory alpinism in the Canadian Rockies. Jon Whyte described Allen as "a haunting figure. Brightly intelligent, active and alert, alive to the nuances of language, a scholar and the finest namer of places the Rockies have ever hosted." Allen was in his freshman year at Yale enrolled in philology (the study of languages) and while in the Rockies Yandell Henderson noted that "He utilized every opportunity to learn words from the Stoney Indians of this region and from these words he developed some of the names that we gave to the peaks." Allen spent most of his spare time attempting to learn the complex nature of the Stoney language.

Allen made his first acquaintance with Lake Louise in the summer of 1891 arriving in a most unconventional way, hiking the 29 km from Field to Laggan rather than via the comforts of the train! His stay at Lake Louise was brief but in that short time he became obsessed with its beauty and unspoiled grandeur. Allen promised himself that he would return after he spent the following year in Europe, during which time he honed his mountaineering skills and climbed the Matterhorn. Sometime later, Allen met another Yale student with similar interests, Walter Wilcox. The two began a close

Four members of the Yale Lake Louise Club (from left to right, Yandell Henderson, Louis Frissell, George Warrington, and Walter Wilcox)

relationship and planned a serious exploration of the Lake Louise region for the summer of 1893.

Reports of Allen's endurance and stamina are legendary. Perhaps his most ambitious adventure occurred on August 11, 1894, when during a single day he completed a trip from a camp in Paradise Valley over Wastach and Wenkchemna Passes, reaching what he described as the "rocky, desolate tree-less valley beyond," called Prospector's Valley. Using a tall limestone pillar called the Eagle's Eyrie as a landmark, Allen reached Opabin Pass at 10 a.m. After naming a number of landmarks he then retraced his route and was back in his Paradise Valley camp by nightfall, completing one of the most remarkable feats of endurance ever recorded in the Rockies.

Later that same year Allen spent six days exploring the region around Lake O'Hara. Allen named many more landmarks at Lake O'Hara using Stoney terms. They rolled off his tongue; Wiwaxy (meaning "high winds"), Yukness ("sharp-pointed peak"), and Oesa ("the lake of ice").

Shortly after receiving his M.A. degree in 1897, at the age of 23, Allen would fall victim to dementia praecox, a form of schizophrenia. He spent the final 40 years of his life in an asylum for the insane.

## Walter Dwight Wilcox (1869–1949)

Walter D. Wilcox, a native of Chicago, was an only son whose father died in a boating accident on Lake Superior when Walter was 10 years old. His mother had historical roots to John Quincy Adams and the family could trace its ancestry back to 1310 in Wales. He entered Yale University, where he received Junior and Senior colloquies and was a member of Alpha Delta Phi. After graduating from Yale in 1893, he studied science in Washington, D.C. and became a proficient writer and photographer. His passion for photography was such that rarely did he climb without his

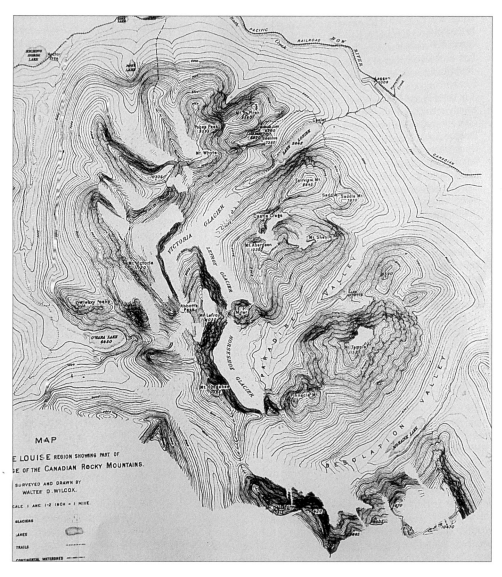

MAP

E LOUISE REGION SHOWING PART OF
SE OF THE CANADIAN ROCKY MOUNTAINS.

SURVEYED AND DRAWN BY
WALTER D. WILCOX.

CALE 1 ANC 1-2 INCH = 1 MILE.

GLACIERS
LAKES
TRAILS
CONTINENTAL WATERSHED

**Map of the Lake Louise region prepared by Walter Wilcox in 1896**

large camera nicknamed "Big Bertha" strapped to his or someone else's unfortunate back. In 1901 he married Annie White Lawson and their only son Dwight Jr., born in 1909, died before his first birthday.

Yandell Henderson has related that "His [Wilcox's] interests were in photography, in which he had great skill and artistic taste, and in geology, particularly in the question whether Lake Louise had been formed by a glacier. He wished to map the lake and its surrounding mountains and to make some ascents of the then virgin peaks." During his many visits to the Rockies, Wilcox completed 20 first ascents. He made the first complete circuit of Mt. Assiniboine in 1895 and almost made the first ascent of the mountain with guide Edward Feuz Jr. in 1901, reaching 11,000 ft. before being turned back, not by difficult conditions but by the inexperience of one of the "amateurs" in the party.

Wilcox was much more than a mountaineer. He was a distinguished Honourary Member of the Alpine Club of Canada, Secretary of the American Alpine Club (1920–1925), President of the Trail Riders of Canada, member of the Royal Geographic Society, and an associated member of the Royal Photographic Society. He was one of the early explorers in the Canadian Rockies whose writings, including *Camping in the Canadian Rockies* (1896), *The Rockies of Canada* (1900), and *Guide to the Lake Louise District* (1909), became classics and did much to bring public attention to the region surrounding Lake Louise. The topographic map of the Lake Louise region he prepared is an elegant, detailed, classic work of art!

## Dr. Yandell Henderson (1874–1944)

Yandell Henderson was born in Louisville Kentucky to an affluent and academic family that included a lawyer, a newspaper owner, a judge, and a dean of a medical school. He only spent one eventful summer, in 1894, in the Rockies, writing an engaging account of it in the 1933 edition of the *Canadian Alpine Journal*. By his own admission, Yandell was not a mountaineer and joined the group only for the adventure and the desire to hunt for Rocky Mountain goats. By default, Henderson became the camp cook. The first breakfast he ever prepared was so bad that the group's Stoney packers protested, "No good eat!" and demanded more pay. Henderson wrote amusingly about his feeble attempt to prepare cornmeal the way his mother taught him, but it only resulted in "five cases of dyspepsia. After forty years, I still remember that stomach-ache."

After graduating from Yale in 1895, Yandell became the most famous and celebrated member of the Yale Club. His destiny was to make important contributions to cardiorespiratory physiology with an emphasis on resuscitation, air pollution, mine safety, and aviation medicine.

After graduating with his B.A., he began studying physiologic chemistry and four years later earned a Ph.D. He became an instructor in physiology at Yale medical school in 1900 and advanced to full professorship in 1911 During World War I, Henderson was chief of the medical section of gas war investigation and became an authority on the pharmacology and toxicology of gasses. Professor Henderson developed refinements for the gas mask and with his associates devised the standard of ventilation for the Holland Tunnel under the Hudson River.

Walter D. Wilcox

## George H. Warrington and Louis F. Frissell

The other two members that formed the Yale Club were George Warrington (1872–1940) and Louis Frissell (1872–1943), classmates at Yale. Both were enthusiastic, well educated, unassuming members of this group of adventurers. Henderson rememberd that "Warrington's chief interests in life were literature and law and secondarily chemistry and geology. He read more and took less physical exercise than any other man that I ever knew in college." Frissell, on the other hand, was more interested in geography and "he wished for adventures and was by nature wholly free from fear of their hazards." After their brief summer of adventure and some might say, misadventure, in 1894, they never returned to the mountains.

Dr. Yandell Henderson

# The Appalachia Mountain Club

Mt. Hector from the viewpoint on the Trans-Canada Highway

scrambles in the Lake Louise region, but Fay, Abbot, and Thompson were after much larger prey. Their goal was a conquest of Mt. Hector (3394 m), up-valley from Laggan.

They hired Tom Wilson to guide them to the base of the mountain and on July 30, 1895, they stood on the summit of the second highest peak yet climbed in the Canadian Rockies. Abbot was none too impressed with the ease of the ascent and in fact wrote of it with some disdain:

*Our party that climbed Mt. Hector cannot, I am afraid, lay claim to much glory therefrom. We had no hair-breath escape; we did not even encounter great hardships except such as are familiar to every bricklayer's apprentice. We did not need to exercise great generalship: the mountain was in plain sight we walked to its base, — some distance, I admit, and not exactly over a paved road, — and then walked until we reached the summit.*

In the summer of 1895, Dr. Charles Fay and R.F. Curtis arrived at Laggan with a large contingent of climbers from the Appalachian Mountain Club. Among this group were Philip S. Abbot and Charles S. Thompson. Abbot was perhaps the most experienced alpinist in America and Thompson was a neophyte, never having climbed before. Most of the club members satisfied themselves with minor

Before leaving Lake Louise the three climbers scrambled to the summit of Mt. Fairview on August 1, where they looked longingly at the glacier capped summit of Mt. Lefroy. Thompson wrote, "our greedy hearts were filled with a desire for its topmost bit of crystal, rock or ice."

# The Swiss Guides

Philip Stanley Abbot's death on Mt. Lefroy in 1896 created a sensation and brought into focus the need for safety in the mountains. Many thought that Abbot's death would be a detriment to climbing in the Rockies, but in fact it only increased the public's interest. When renowned Swiss guide Peter Sarbach was hired to lead the Anglo-American party of climbers to the summit of Mt. Lefroy on the anniversary of Abbot's death the following year, a new age of mountaineering was born in the Canadian Alps.

The value of a trained guide became apparent to the management of the CPR. If they were to entice more visitors to the mountains, then the mountains would have to become a safer place for their clientele, and who better to lead them than qualified Swiss guides. In 1899, amid much fanfare, two of Switzerland's foremost guides, Edward Feuz Sr. and Christian Hasler Sr., arrived at Glacier House in the Selkirk Mtns.

The Swiss guides not only added safety but they also brought a different attitude to the Rockies. Bob Sandford expressed it best:

*With them they brought significant evolutions in mountaineering technique garnered from long experience in the Alps. But, perhaps, more importantly, they brought an attitude about mountains and a disposition towards climbing that would gradually change the way many Canadians would think about their own summits. The Swiss had a reverence for the alpine that would gradually permeate the fabric of Canadian culture.*

Edward Feuz Sr. (left) and Christian Hasler Sr. (right), the first Swiss Guides

The second generation of Swiss guides gradually followed and their headquarters became Lake Louise. Alpinism in the Canadian Rockies entered a new era. Six of these guides are especially noteworthy: Edward Feuz Jr. (1884–1981); Rudolph Aemmer (1883–1973); Christian Hasler Jr. (1889–1942); Walter Feuz (1894–1985); Ernest Feuz (1889–1960); and Walter Perren (1914–1967), the last Swiss guide to be hired (in 1950).

The Swiss guides would lead clients from around the world to the top of nearly every major peak in the Rockies. They amassed a record of first ascents never again to be equalled in the Rockies, leading clients on the first ascents of 396 major peaks in the Rockies.

# Guardians of the Valley

Mt. Temple  Fairview Mtn.  Haddo Pk.  Mt. Aberdeen  Mt. Lefroy

Saddle Mtn.  Sheol Mtn.  Haddo Pk.  Mt. Aberdeen  Fairview Mtn.

Top  A panoramic view of Lake Louise peaks from Herbert Lake on the Icefields Parkway

Bottom: Peaks above Lake Louise

## Fairview Mtn. 2744 m and Saddle Mtn. 2420 m

The panoramic view of the Saddle-back is familiar to everyone who has entered the townsite of Lake Louise from the turnoff on the Trans-Canada Highway. Yandell Henderson hiked to this alp on July18, 1883 and it seems that he was the source of the names used to describe this high alpine valley above Lake Louise. Henderson recalled "a beautiful pass or alp between two mountain tops which I have named the 'Saddle.' " The diminutive peak to the right of this pass has been officially named Saddle Mtn., while Henderson's beautiful alp is known as the Saddle-back.

The triangular peak overlooking the lake and the town of Lake Louise has been officially named Mt. Fairview because of the splendid views it affords in all directions from its summit. Initially, the slopes of Mt. Fairview were apparently once home to a large contingent of mountain goats, which led Wilcox and Allen to call the peak Goat Mtn.

## Sheol Mtn. 2779 m

In Hebrew, *Sheol* is the abode of the dead or, in other translations, another name for the underworld or hell. Allen christened the peak with this name and said it was because of the "gloomy appearance" he thought inherent in the desolate valley he saw below the mountain. The name led Jon Whyte to muse, "it's a nice

philological joke that 'Sheol' should guard the way to Paradise (Paradise Valley)."

## Haddo Pk. 3070 m

It is only fitting the Haddo Pk. should lie next to Mt. Aberdeen, as Haddo House was the ancestral home of the Earl of Aberdeen. Haddo House dates back to 1731 when William Adam designed the residence for the second Earl of Aberdeen. However, the actual name commemorates Lord Haddo, the eighth Earl of Aberdeen.

## Mt. Aberdeen 3151 m

Mt. Aberdeen was the first mountain climbed in the Lake Louise area (by the Yale Lake Louise Club) and was originally named Mt. Hazel by Walter Wilcox in 1896. It was renamed in 1897 to commemorate Sir John Campbell Hamilton Gordon (1847–1934), the seventh Earl of Aberdeen and Governor General of Canada from 1893 to 1898. His grandfather George (1784–1860), the fourth Earl of Aberdeen, had negotiated the Oregon Treaty with the United States, which settled the boundary dispute between Canada and the United States over the Oregon Territory.

Even before coming to Canada to serve as Governor General, Lord Aberdeen had fallen in love with the country. During his world tour in 1890, he purchased a ranch in the Okanagan Valley, naming it "Guisachan" after Lady Aberdeen's father's estate in Scotland. Lord Aberdeen was Governor General of Canada during a period of political transition and an era marred by conflicting issues ranging from separate French schools in Manitoba to the completion of the transcontinental railroad. He and his wife Ishbel Maria Majoribanks (see Mt. Isbehl, page TK) were genuinely interested in the well being of all Canadians and together they travelled extensively throughout the country. He took an interest in the welfare of the people of the First Nations and was rewarded by being made an honourary chief of both the Six Nations and Blackfoot people. Lord Aberdeen will be remembered for transforming the role of the office of Governor General from that of an aristocrat representing the king or queen of England to a symbol representing the interests of all Canadian citizens. After his term as Governor General, Lord Aberdeen

Haddo House, Scotland

Sir John Campbell, the seventh Earl of Aberdeen

Mt. Temple

Mt. Aberdeen
Sheol Mtn.
Haddo Pk.
Saddle Mtn.

View of peaks from Morant's Curve on the Bow Valley Parkway

returned to the United Kingdom where he served as Lord Lieutenant of Ireland.

## Mt. Temple 3543 m

Mt. Temple is often called the "Eiger of the Canadian Rockies" because of its incredible "mile-high" north face. Perhaps Allen's impression of Mr. Temple, read before the Appalachian Club on March 12, 1895, best summarizes a first view of this magnificent peak:

> One who travels west from Banff up the valley of the Bow will see in front of him, shortly after leaving Cascade Siding, a tall helmet-shaped peak rising in a series of inaccessible cliffs to a snow-tipped summit. But it is not until Laggan [Lake Louise] is reached, and the western face of the peak is seen — now to the southeast — that its height or beauty is adequately realized, although from all points it dominates the landscape. From a base fifteen hundred feet higher than Lag-

gan, this western face rises in one unbroken wall nearly four thousand feet. A plateau above the latter is occupied by a magnificent area of glacier and neve, sweeping down in curving folds from the summit to the top of the wall, while the overhanging seracs above, and the fine powder on the scattered ledges below tell of many a thundering avalanche of this ice. This is Mount Temple.

Mt. Temple, the monarch of the Bow Range and the highest peak in the region, was named by George Dawson in 1884 in honour of Sir Richard Temple (1826–1902). Richard Temple joined the Bengal Civil Service and, after admirable service, was appointed Lieutenant-Governor of Bombay. After his service there, he returned to England in 1883 and began another facet of his political career. Temple was also a noted economist who visited the Rocky Mountains in 1884 as the leader of the British Association for the Advancement of Science.

# On Top of Their World

Labels on image: Mt. Temple; Mt. Allen; Mt. Tuzo; Deltaform Mtn.

amuel Allen was obsessed with climbing this mountain ever since he first viewed the peak from the summit of Devil's Thumb in 1891. When he and Wilcox were forced to abort their attempt on the peak in 1893 it only aroused his passion. The peak had to be his! The following year, on August 18, Allen, Wilcox, and Frissell made their way in the darkness to Sentinel Pass from where they assaulted the peak.

Wilcox described their ascent in the following manner:

*The outlook from the pass was indeed discouraging. Cliffs and ledges with broken stones amid loose debris seemed to oppose all safe passage. Fortunately, as we progressed the difficulties vanished, and not till we reached an altitude of about 10,000 feet did we encounter any real obstacles. We found a passage through the great rock wall, which had defeated us last year, by the aid of a little gully, which, however, entailed some rather difficult climbing. This arduous work continued throughout the next 1,000 feet, when, at an altitude of 11,000, we came to the great slope between the southwest and west arêtes and found an easy passage to the summit.*

A rugged view from the summit of Fairview Mtn.

Allen had just realized his dream and Mt. Temple became the first peak over 3355 m (11,000 ft.) to be climbed in the Canadian Rockies. Today their route is deemed the "tourist route," a popular scramble. In 1894 it was the top of their world and Wilcox was euphoric and reported, "Many a hearty cheer rent the thin air as our little party of three reached the summit, for we were standing where no man had ever stood before, and, if I mistake not, at the highest altitude yet reached in North America north of the United States boundary."

# The Temple Tragedy

Mt. Temple is the ultimate scramble in the Canadian Rockies. Each year the "tourist route" attracts hundreds of avid scramblers with hopes of standing on the summit of this majestic peak. This so-called tourist route is not one to be taken lightly and on

Monday, July 11, 1955 became the site of the worst-ever mountaineering accident in Canadian history. What follows is a story of an incredible tragedy. It is the story of an event that would forever change the lives of 16 teenaged boys from the Wilderness Club of Philadelphia. Seven

Mt. Temple     "Little Temple"

Two views of Mt. Temple: the north face (left) and the east face (right)

would perish on the mountain in this terrible tragedy.

The fateful day began with the excitement and anticipation of scrambling to the summit of the highest peak in the Lake Louise region. Their leader, William H. Oeser, had chosen the popular tourists route for their ascent. Under proper conditions, this route is neither difficult nor hazardous but caution, common sense, and assessment of avalanche conditions are paramount. None of the party seemed prepared for the conditions that can be encountered, and should be expected, at high altitude. They were wearing only light summer clothing. Some of the boys had crampons but others were clad in baseball cleats. The route was unfamiliar to everyone in the party. A disaster was in the making.

After reaching about 2600 m, Oeser, together with five of the boys, dropped out to take pictures, leaving the remaining lads under the leadership of William Watts and Tony Woodfield, both 16 years old. Conditions were anything but safe as they worked their way over and across snow-covered slopes. Ricky Ballard, a young survivor of the accident, would later testify, "We could hear avalanches all around us." They reached about 2900 m late in the afternoon (4:00 p.m.) when they decided that a retreat would be most prudent in the face of the dangerous conditions.

In order to safely cross a snowfield they tied two-inch manila ropes together to form a single line approximately 30 m in length and then roped up at 2-m intervals. Watts assumed the lead while Woodfield acted as the anchor. Just as they were crossing the slope they heard the noise that strikes fear in the heart of every climber. Avalanche! Woodfield dug his ice axe into the slope in an attempt to arrest the fall but within seconds they were engulfed by snow and their slender, useless manila rope snapped, sending 10 of the boys tumbling down the mountainside in a heap of bodies, rocks, and snow. Only good fortune saved Woodfield as he held on for dear life. Miraculously, the avalanche stopped after careening about 100 m down the slope just before entering a narrow funnel and a drop off over another cliff.

Thirteen-year-old Peter Smith felt the rope tighten around his neck, threatening to strangle him, but somehow managed to pull free from his entrapment. Tony Woodfield scrambled down the slope to find Smith almost unscathed, Fred Ballard (13 years old) dazed from a scalp wound, Jerry Chattenburg (14) severely injured about the head, and

Luther Seddon suffering from a broken leg. Four others, David Chappin, Miles Marble, and the two Balis twins, had been either completely or partially buried by the avalanche. Smith was immediately dispatched down the mountain to obtain help. Hearing a cry for help, Woodfield used his shoes and ice axe to dig Watts from beneath a foot of snow.

Meanwhile, group leader William Oeser had followed the progress of his protegés high up on the peak and had witnessed some unusual activity but decided that the boys were just "fooling around." Only after being alerted by cries for help from a hysterical Peter Smith did he realize that a tragedy had occurred and he immediately started up the mountain. When Oeser reached the site of the accident Woodfield was hysterical and probably suffering from shock, at which point Oeser sent him back down the slope while he tried to rescue the remaining boys.

It was 5:00 p.m. before Woodfield and Smith reached park officials at Moraine Lake and alerted them of the accident.

Wardens Wes Gilstrof and Jack Schuarte, together with Lake Louise house physician Dr. Sutton, set off from Moraine Lake to investigate the scene in advance of a major rescue party from Banff. When they reached the avalanche site they found the situation even more desperate as a light freezing drizzle had begun to fall and the boys were in danger of perishing from exposure. A dazed and severely injured Fred Ballard started to descend the mountain but one of the Balis twins was too severely hurt to be moved. Wes Gilstrof hoisted Chattenburg on his back and began stumbling down the ice-crusted snow, leaving Schuarte to do what he could at the scene.

The major rescue party of some 20 men, led by Chief Warden Bert Pittaway, Walter Perren, and Jerry Campbell, arrived from Banff and left Moraine Lake at 7:30 p.m. with baskets and extra clothing, along with climbing and rescue equipment. Their fast pace forced some members of the rescue party to drop out from sheer exhaustion but every second was vital to the survival of the boys. In the gathering darkness they met an utterly exhausted Gilstrof stumbling down the slope with Chattenburg on his back. Pittaway ordered Gilstrof to leave Chattenburg to the care of other members of the rescue party and "to return and lead us to the scene." It was a cruel thing to impose on the exhausted Gilstrof but only he knew the location of the accident site. They would have to find it in the darkness aided only by flashlights.

Retracing his steps, Gilstrof led Perren and Pittaway back up the mountain and together they reached the accident scene in complete darkness around 11:30 p.m. Jack Schuarte had made progress in uncovering the avalanche victims, but exposure had already taken the lives of all of the boys except one of the Balis twins and he succumbed to his injuries just as they prepared to lift him onto a stretcher. It was then that Perren realized that two of the boys were still missing. A frantic search to find them ensued in the hope that they would still be alive. Walter Perren returned to where he had uncovered the half-buried body of William Watts and followed the bloodstained "climbing" rope in an attempt to find the two missing boys. At 3:00 a.m. the next day, the frozen rope led him to the bodies of William Wise (15) and Miles Marble (12) buried beneath over a half metre of snow. Later, it was determined that Wise had died instantly from head injuries while Marble perished from shock and hypothermia.

Perren decided that the bodies had to be brought down that night due to the "high avalanche hazard during the day." The darkness, the snow and ice from the drizzle, and the exhaustion of the rescue party combined to create hazardous conditions for the descent, but four hours later, at 7:00 a.m., Tuesday, July 12, the worst tragedy ever to occur on Mt. Temple was brought to a tearful conclusion. Later, at the inquest, Coroner M.M. Cantor concluded that the boys were ill-prepared for such a climb, lacked knowledge of the mountain, and were the victims of their own youthful enthusiasm and inexperience.

# Cathedrals, Pinnacles, and Towers

Mt. Hungabee

The spectacular pinnacles at Sentinel Pass

A high col separates Mt. Temple from the peak to the west. Samuel Allen and Yandell Henderson reached this col during their reconnaissance and decided that Sentinel Pass would be an appropriate name for the pass due to the presence of the spectacular pinnacles near its summit. Wilcox, on the other hand seemed to think that the name of the pass was "so called from a small gendarme near the top vividly recalling a human figure as seen from Paradise Valley." He was of course referring to the "Grand Sentinel," the largest of the pinnacles. Whatever the correct version, Allen named the peak immediately west of the pass Sentinel Mountain on account of these spectacular obelisks, and to the south across a broad snow pass, "was a sharp peak, which we called Cathedral … " Sadly, only the pass retains Allen's original name, while the Grand Sentinel has been reserved for the spectacular obelisk on the north side of Pinnacle Mtn.

After their ascent of Mt. Temple, when they were back in the safety of Paradise Valley, Allen was able to reflect upon their accomplishment: "I paused upon the grass-slopes to admire the sunset glow upon Mount Temple, lighting its summit with crimson and silver. The ice-slopes of the Sentinel glowed like molten metal, save where the great black aiguilles, rising like watch-towers from the shining surface, cast long shadows on the ice." No one could have said it more eloquently!

## Pinnacle Mtn. 3067 m

Allen's Sentinel Mtn., lying 2 km southwest of Mt. Temple, is now Pinnacle Mtn., a name ascribed to it by Walter Wilcox. In 1909 Edward Feuz Jr., Rudolph Aemmer, and J.W.A. Hickson had the honour of being the first to step on its summit after the peak had repelled three previous attacks by the leading guides of the day.

Pinnacle Mtn. is notorious for its rotten rock. Before being enticed by Hickson to try the peak again, Edward Feuz Jr. was heard to exclaim, "I won't try that wretched peak again." But he indeed did try again and after some serious climbing on treacherous rock the trio reached the crux of the climb, a black limestone

tower of some 300 vertical ft. covered with ice and a precipitous 2,000-ft. drop-off into Paradise Valley. Hickson began to wonder why he was there and assessed their situation as being "very much in the position of flies on a nearly vertical wall covered with sand which from time to time was crumbling off." Fortunately, Feuz found holds "an inch or two wide and a few inches long on a part of which a nailed-boot edge could obtain a transitory grip." Nerves frayed, they toiled on this tower for two hours before finally reaching a saddle below the summit, at which point Feuz turned to Hickson and said, "I think we've got him." They reached the summit at 2:30 p.m. after spending over eight hours ascending the peak.

Pinnacle Mtn. wasn't about to forgive the ascent party for this apparent insult to its character and had another surprise in store for their descent. Unwilling to retrace their precarious ascent route, the guides decided a route on the backside of the peak would be a more judicious choice. Hickson recounted the following:

*At the corner or angle where the ledge we were on terminated there was a peculiar arrangement of rock which had resulted in the formation of a small square hole with nothing but sky to be seen on the further side. Under this*

*hole there was a gap in the ledge of about three feet, with a drop of about fifteen feet into a dark pit below. To cross the gap it was necessary to lie down flat on the ledge on the one side with face to the rock, stretch your feet to the rock on the other, your body thus spanning the gap, then draw yourself through the hole and gradually swing yourself into an upright position by the help of the rope and the handholds in the further wall of the rock.*

They overcame that obstacle and in doing so avoided the problems encountered on the black tower. Later, Swiss guides placed a wire cable to which a large rope was permanently attached on the face so that "in future it would be less dangerous."

## Eiffel Pk. 3084 m and Eiffel Tower 3080 m

This is just another example of why some consider the Rockies the worst-named peaks in the world. The Geographic Board of Canada shunned Allen's original name, Cathedral, in favour of this name, which has no significant meaning to the history of the region. Apparently someone thought the peak bore a resemblance to the tower built by Gustave Eiffel for the Paris Exposition of 1889.

Left: Pinnacle Mtn. from Mt. Temple

Right: Eiffel Pk. and Eiffel Tower from the slopes of Mt. Temple

# Moraine Lake and the Valley of the Ten Peaks

Mt. Little
Mt. Tonsa
Mt. Perren
Mt. Allen
Mt. Tuzo
Deltaform Mtn.

Moraine Lake and the Valley of the Ten Peaks from the Rockpile

"No scene has ever given me an equal impression of inspiring solitude and rugged grandeur. I stood on a great stone of the moraine where, from a slight elevation, a magnificent view of the lake lay before me, and while studying the details of this unknown and unvisited spot, spent the happiest half-hour of my life." That is how Walter Wilcox described the magical setting of Moraine Lake in 1905, six years after he and Ross Peacock had "discovered" the lake.

## Moraine Lake

Moraine Lake rivals Lake Louise in beauty and setting, although the closeness of the rugged peaks around the lake does give one a claustrophobic feeling. The U-shaped valley and the mountains rimming it were carved by ancient glaciers. Wenkchemna Glacier at the head of the valley is the remaining remnant of that icy period in the valley's past.

In 1899 Walter Wilcox and Ross Peacock began to explore Wenkchemna Valley and made the first visit to the shores of the lake. From the top of the Rockpile they discovered a most splendid sight, "a narrow, secluded valley with a small lake enclosed by wild rugged precipices ... one of the most beautiful lakes I have ever seen." Wilcox mistakenly believed that the huge rock pile, upon which he was standing, was a glacial moraine and named the lake after that geological feature.

Geologists now believe that a massive rock avalanche from the slopes of Mt. Babel produced the rock pile and not a glacial moraine as Wilcox had surmised. These huge blocks of quartzite were probably deposited in the middle of the valley by a gigantic rock avalanche off the slopes of Mt. Babel. They are not just any quartzite blocks, but Gog quartzite, the oldest and hardest rock in this part of the Rocky Mountains! Another possibility is that that these boulders are the result of a rockslide farther up the valley. The boulders rode the surface of the advancing glacier, to be deposited at their present location when the glacier began to retreat thousands of years ago.

## Moraine Lake Facts

Around 1900 Tom Wilson cut the first trail from Lake Louise to Moraine Lake. In 1902 the CPR improved the trail and before long a road to accommodate carriages was built. The first road to accommodate cars was completed in 1921. The CPR constructed the first teahouse at the lake

Nom Yamnee Tonsa Shappee Sagowa Sagnowa Sapta Neptuak

in 1912. It underwent many modifications until the current lodge and guest buildings were completed in 1990. In 1983 the Alpine Club of Canada built the Neil Colgan Hut, on the col between Mts. Little and Bowlen (at the highest altitude in Canada for a permanent structure). One Hollywood film, *Saskatchewan*, was filmed on the shores of Moraine Lake in 1953.

Moraine Lake and the Valley of the Ten Peaks with the original Stoney names bestowed by Samuel Allen

# Wenkchemna: The Valley of the Ten Peaks

In 1893, from a shoulder high on the eastern slopes of Mt. Temple, Walter Wilcox and Samuel Allen first set eyes on this valley. It was a dreary, bitterly cold and overcast day rent with snow showers; this only added to the austere setting. As Wilcox peered through the gloom, he was overwhelmed by the utter desolation of a valley dominated by rock and ice. The valley was completely "destitute of vegetation or any green thing, filled with glaciers

and vast heaps of moraine, and the slides of debris from the adjacent mountain side. All was desolate, gloomy, cold and monotonous in colour ..." Wilcox called it Desolation Valley. Allen thought otherwise and described it best:

*The region to the S., with mountains wonderfully sharp and of great height, and quite unlocated upon Dr. Dawson's Reconnaissance Map, and with*

Mt. Tonsa | Mt. Perren | Mt. Allen | Mt. Tuzo | Deltaform Mtn.

**Peaks Four through Nine from the trail to Sentinel Pass**

*which I have since become well acquainted, was still an-unnamed, unmapped, untrodden fairy land, a bewildering and seemingly endless range of rocky peaks and shining glaciers. I can still recall the thrill from the splendours of this then ideal scene ...*

The next summer, in preparation for their assault on Mt. Temple, Allen and Yandell Henderson scrambled to the summit of Sentinel Pass from which they were able to determine the extent of the valley with its hidden treasure. Allen recalled the scene:

*From the top, which we finally reached, 8,950 ft. above the sea, two small green lakes were visible just beneath us, fed by the snow-fields on this side of the pass. These I named Minnes-timma, or sleeping water. The valley beyond was the one into which I had looked from Mount Temple in the summer of 1893.*

Allen continued to describe the valley in detail:

*I afterwards saw that it was bounded on the E. by a superb range of ten sharp peaks, to which I applied the Indian numerals from one to ten. Upon descending the pass I saw at the base of No. 1, Mount Heejee a grand and gloomy lake, reflecting in its dark surface the walls and hanging glaciers of Mount Heejee. This lake, which I named Heejee, I had photographed the previous summer at the base of Mount Temple.*

How did the name Wenkchemna come about? Standing on the summit of Mt. Temple in 1894 with Wilcox and Henderson, Allen was speechless: the view remained "a task beyond my powers of description." However, never really at a loss for words, and in the eloquent fashion only he was capable of, Allen wrote, "From the east the eye sweeps over the ten sharp rock-peaks of the crest, separated from each other by slender precipitous couloirs of ice, which from the eastern boundary of the valley east of Mt. Temple, which I have called by its Assiniboine [Stoney] equivalent Wenkchemna, or the Valley of the Ten Peaks."

Allen and Henderson explored much of the upper reaches of the Wenkchemna Valley before returning to their camp in Paradise Valley via another pass farther to the west, which Allen christened Wastach, Stoney for "beautiful" or "wonderful."

Allen decided to name each of the ten peaks using the Stoney numerals from one to ten. In an article written in 1894, Allen refers to "ten sharp peaks, to which I applied the Indian numerals from one to ten. Upon descending the pass [Sentinel Pass] I saw at the base of No.1, Mount Heejee, a grand and gloomy lake, reflecting in its dark surface the walls and hanging glaciers of Mount Heejee."

# The Ten Peaks

*Rounding a corner of the hill, we had a sudden and most striking view of Moraine Lake and the magnificent range of the Ten Peaks, with their tremendous precipices. rising beyond .. Not even Lake Louise can boast of so noble a galaxy of guardian mountains as is furnished by the range of The Ten Peaks and the craggy and imposing pile of Mount Temple.*

Mt. Babel, Bident Mtn., Mt. Quadra, Mt. Fay, Mt. Little, Mt. Bowlen

These were the remarks of Hugh Stutfield and J. Norman Collie when they entered this valley in 1902; they could be the impressions of any visitor to the lake today, over one hundred years later. Little has changed since that time and an almost identical view awaits you as you cross the shoulder of Mt. Temple on the road to Moraine Lake.

## Mt. Fay 3234 m

Mt. Fay was named in honour of Dr. Charles Ernest Fay (1346–1931), Professor of Modern Languages at Tufts University and perhaps the most distinguished North American alpinist of his day. Fay was born on March 10 in Roxbury, Massachusetts to Reverend Cyrus H. Fay, pastor of a local Universalist Church, and his wife Anne Hyne Fay. Religious, self-disciplined, and intelligent, Charles graduated from Tufts College in 1868 and was later appointed full professor after earning his masters degree in 1877 and an Honourary Doctor of Letters in 1900.

As his interest in mountaineering grew, he chaired the meeting that founded the Appalachian Mountain Club, the first mountaineering club in North America. Fay served as its president for four terms and as editor of its historical journal

*Appalachia,* for more than 40 years. Content to climb in the mountains of New England, Fay would be 40 years of age before being introduced to the "big" peaks in Colorado and California. In 1890 he made his first trip to the Canadian Alps, a trek he would make more than 20 times. In 1895 his mountaineering life was to change forever when he met a young graduate of Harvard Law School and

Top: Peaks from the road to Moraine Lake.

Bottom: Professor Charles Fay

Mt. Fay

Mt. Little

Mt. Bowlen

Mt. Tonsa

Peaks One through Four from the trail to Sentinel Pass

an experienced mountaineer, Philip Stanley Abbot.

Fay spent an engaging summer in 1895 with Philip Abbot and Charles Thompson as he was introduced to a dazzling new world of ice and snow on the virgin summit of Mt. Hector (3394 m), scrambled to the summit of Mt. Stephen, and tramped up various peaks in Rogers Pass. He had experienced his "Rocky Mountain High" and would return numerous times and become part of the history of the region. A solid but short friendship with Abbot ensued as an elated Fay retreated from the Rockies to plan new ascents for the following fateful year that was to become legendary in the history of Canadian mountaineering (see Mt. Lefroy, page 92). On August 3, 1897, the anniversary of Abbot's death, Fay was present for the first ascent of Mt. Lefroy. Two days later he made the first ascent of Mt. Victoria. In all, Professor Charles Ernest Fay would complete 14 first ascents in the Canadian Alps.

It was a great honour for Fay when the Geographic Board of

Christian Kaufmann

Canada allowed him to choose Peak #1 (Heejee) in the Valley of the Ten Peaks to be named after him in recognition of his achievements. Now, only one final task remained; to complete the first ascent of "his" mountain. In the summer of 1904, Fay engaged Hans Kaufmann to guide him to his goal. Unknown to Fay, Gertrude Benham had contracted Christian Kaufmann, brother of Hans, for that same purpose. The two brothers had chosen two different routes for the ascents but the route chosen by Hans, over the protestations of Fay, proved to be too difficult and they had to retreat. Christian, on the other hand, led Benham up an easy route to claim the first ascent of the peak on July 20, thereby depriving Fay of the prize he so cherished.

Christian Kaufmann (1872–1939) first came to Canada as one of Edward Whymper's accomplished Swiss guides in the summer of 1901. He has been described as tall and handsome, with a cheerful and engaging personality, and superior skills on a mountain. James Outram was impressed with his skills; he was "a magnificent rock-climber and it was a treat to watch the skill and science he displayed." Christian even had the distinction of guiding Sir Winston Churchill to the summit of the Wetterhorn in 1894 (long before Churchill became famous). His 42 first ascents in the Rockies are small testament to his skills.

Christian and his brother Hans were perhaps unfairly blamed for the unfortunate set of circumstances surrounding the Mt. Fay controversy.

Many in the climbing community suspected treachery on their part, including Swiss guide Edward Feuz Jr. who was furious over this "dirty trick." According to Feuz:

*Christian knew the country. He'd been there with an American named Allen, who had made a map, and climbed several of those peaks. Those he hadn't climbed, Mount Fay included, he'd seen from Deltaform across the way, and he knew exactly how to find the easiest way up. Both brothers thought it would be a great joke to fool old man Fay.*

Such was the deep-seated anger some members of the guiding fraternity felt about this unfortunate set of circumstances. Fay was disappointed and bitter to say the least and he never forgave the Kaufmann brothers for this apparent act of indiscretion. When the officials at the CPR heard of this deed the Kaufmann brothers were relieved of their duties and never again guided in Canada for the CPR.

Charles Fay did return to make the second ascent of Mt. Fay on August 5, but sadly it virtually brought his climbing career to an end. Professor Charles E. Fay died of complications after undergoing surgery for appendicitis on January 25, 1931.

## Mt. Little 3140 m

Professor George Thomas Little (1857–1915) was Librarian of Bowdoin College in Maine and an active member of the American Alpine Club. He was second on the rope connected to Philip Abbot on that fateful day on Mt. Lefroy. Originally, this was Peak #2 or *Nom* on Allen's map of the Ten Peaks. In 1901 he returned to the Valley of the Ten Peaks and completed the first ascent of the mountain named in his honour, as well as that of Mt. Bowlen.

## Mt. Bowlen 3072 m

In 1953 the peak Allen had named Yamnee, or Peak #3, was officially renamed to pay homage to John James Bowlen (1876–1959), Alberta's longest serving Lieutenant-Governor. Born in Prince Edward Island, Bowlen purchased a farm in Saskatchewan in 1906, and a ranch near Rosebud, Alberta in 1910 where he raised horses. He next purchased the Q Ranch on the Alberta – Saskatchewan border, along the international boundary, which had a range of approximately 100,000 acres. Bowlen sold this ranch in 1920 and purchased yet another naming it the Nine-Bar. It would eventually become the largest horse ranch in Canada.

Bowlen was defeated in his first attempt at federal politics in the general election of 1914 but finally, in 1930, he won election to the Alberta Legislature and represented Calgary as a Liberal MLA for 14 years. In 1950 he was appointed Lieutenant-Governor of Alberta, a post he served until his death in office in 1959.

Top: Peaks above Moraine Lake from near Coral Creek picnic area on the Bow Valley Parkway

Bottom: The Honourable J.J. Bowlen

Mt. Babel    Mt. Fay    Mt. Bowlen    Mt. Tonsa

Early morning from
Larch Valley

## Mt. Tonsa 3054 m

Mt. Tonsa, Peak #4, is one of the few peaks in the valley that retains the original name bestowed on it by Samuel Allen.

## Mt. Perren 3051 m

Samuel Allen's Peak #5 (Sapta) was renamed in 1968 to honour the distinguished career of Walter Perren (1914–1967), a Swiss guide from Zermatt, who later became the Chief Warden of Banff National Park. Perren will be forever known for founding the National Parks Rescue School.

Walter Perren was born in Switzerland on January 13, 1914, the son of a mountain climber and the grandson of one of the first to climb the Matterhorn. He had 144 ascents of the Matterhorn to his credit before coming to Canada in 1950 at the age of 36. Perren was perhaps the finest climber of all the Swiss guides and even the renowned Edward Feuz Jr. acknowledged that he couldn't do as well as Walter; quite a compliment from a legend of the Canadian

Rockies. He never signed a summit register and abhorred the phrase "to conquer a peak." To him mountains were sacred places just as they were to the Stoneys. Once on Mt. Victoria he pointed out the phenomenon called the Brocken Spectre to his friend Jim Sime and commented, "See how close we are to God, Jim."

Walter joined the National Park Service in May 1955, later becoming Chief Warden of the Parks Mountaineering Service. He then became concerned about the increasing number of accidents in the Canadian Alps and organized a Mountain Rescue School called Cuthead College, of which he was the primary instructor.

It came as a shock to the mountain community when in 1967, this little man with boundless energy and incomparable climbing skills, and who considered mountain tops sacred places died of leukemia. This mountain and the park's rescue service live as a legacy to Walter Perren, the last of the CPR's famous Swiss guides.

## Mt. Allen 3310 m

One has to wonder if Samuel Evans Stokes Allen (1874–1945) would have approved of renaming the peak he called Shappee, Peak #6, after him. An exceptionally brilliant man, much of the nomenclature of Lake Louise, Paradise Valley, Moraine Lake, and Lake O'Hara owe their origins to this tragic figure. An enthusiastic and competent mountaineer, he ascended the Matterhorn and 13 of the highest peaks in the Austrian Tyrol before commencing his pioneering explorations in the region around Lake Louise (see Chapter 9 for more on Allen's exploits). Of all the early literature written about the Canadian Alps, none compare to the locution, eloquence, and poetic style of this brilliant scholar.

Born in Philadelphia to parents of Welsh and English ancestry, he was privileged to receive an education at the best private schools before enrolling at Yale University where he majored in philology (the study of languages). He was one of the youngest, if not the most intellectual member of his class Allen graduated Phi Beta Kappa in 1894 and obtained an M.A. degree in 1897.

He was a deeply religious man, who upon graduation began studying for the degree of Doctor of Philosophy, intending to enter the ministry of the Protestant Episcopal Church. Allen's bouts with schizophrenia prevented the realization of this goal. His death from pneumonia complicated by kidney failure, after confinement in a mental institution for more than 40 years, gave release to a brilliant but clouded mind whose only memories were of the beloved mountains of his youth.

**Samuel E.S. Allen**

## Mt. Tuzo 3245 m

Samuel Allen's Peak #7 (Sagowa) has since been renamed Mt. Tuzo in honour of Henrietta Tuzo Wilson (1873–1955), a woman who loved the mountains and mountaineering. She is one of those remarkable individuals with a storied ancestral past who added to the fame of her already famous family tree. Henrietta Tuzo, or "Hettie" as she became known, was born in Victoria, B.C. on May 6, 1873 and came from a line of distant Angevin Huguenot ancestors who landed in Virginia in the 17th century. Her father, H.A. Tuzo, was one of British Columbia's pioneer medical doctors. He had joined the Hudson's Bay Company as a clerk and had had the privilege of crossing the Athabasca Pass in 1853 with none other than Sir George Simpson.

She became interested in mountain climbing and her first climbing experience occurred in the Tyrols in 1896 where she climbed the Ortler (3902 m). In 1898, on her way to visit her only brother in Nelson, B.C., Hettie discovered Banff and immediately fell in love with the mountains.

As her ascents in the Canadian Rockies and the Selkirk Mtns. continued to mount, so did her stature as a climber. In 1906 she became a founding member of the Alpine Club of Canada.

On July 21, 1906 Hettie realized a dream few individuals experience; with guide Christian Kaufmann, she made the first ascent of the peak that would be named in her honour. The ascent went without incident and after a nap on the summit they began a descent that would almost

Mt. Allen

Mt. Tuzo

Deltaform Mtn.

Panorama of Mts. Allen and Tuzo, and Deltaform Mtn, from Larch Valley

end both of their careers. Hearing a report, they were barely able to scramble to a position of safety as a huge rock avalanche wiped out their tracks! Coincidentally, it was the last of the Ten Peaks to be "conquered."

Hettie met her future husband, John Armistead Wilson, in Banff that same year and they were married in England on November 14, 1907. After her marriage, Hettie never returned to her mountain climbing exploits as she and her husband moved to Ottawa where she became active in civic affairs. They had three children – John Tuzo, Mary Loetitia, and William Henry Tuzo. In the storied tradition of her family, eldest son John graduated from Princeton with a Ph.D. in geophysics. His theoretical work became instrumental to the formation of the theory of continental drift, a theory that would eventually lead to the explanation of the formation of the mountains his mother had climbed!

## Deltaform Mtn. 3424 m

Samuel Allen named this Peak #8 or Saknowa. Wilcox preferred the name Deltaform because its northerly face reminded him of the shape of the Greek letter "delta." In 1898 Deltaform Mtn.became the official name.

A. Eggers, H.C. Parker, and the Kaufmann brothers completed the first ascent on September 1, 1903, but it was the second ascent in 1909 that proved to be the most exciting. On the anniversary of the first ascent, H.W.A. Hickson, Rudolph Aemmer, and Edward Feuz Jr. began an ascent that almost ended in catastrophe. After three hours of steady climbing, a chimney some 40 ft. in height with few good holds and lots of loose debris was encountered and had to be surmounted. Hickson recounted the following:

Deltaform Mtn.

Neptuak Mtn.

*Aemmer, who entered the chimney first and had cleared away most of the rubbish was well towards the top and waiting for Feuz to follow when, although exercising great caution, he dislodged a good-sized stone, which, crashing down, inflicted a severe wound on the back of Feuz's head ... Blood poured down over Feuz's face and neck, and concluding that the climb was at an end I considered on how we could get down again.*

After Feuz regained his senses, he would hear nothing about a retreat, and pulling himself together joined Aemmer at the top of the chimney.

The summit pinnacle was reached some hours later but only after a second chimney was overcome when Aemmer was forced to stand on Feuz's shoulders to obtain enough of a handhold to pull himself out of the obstacle. Without delay, Aemmer led the way to a "very disintegrated top, which culminates in two pinnacles covered with smooth, white, weather-worn limestone rocks. It was now 1:40 p.m." and the climb had taken eight hours to complete.

## Neptuak Mtn. 3237 m

This is another of the peaks named by Samuel Allen that still retains its original Stoney name, Neptuak, or Peak #9. On Thursday, September 2, 1902, J. Norman Collie, Hugh E.M. Stutfield, G.M. Weed, H. Woolley, and Christian Kaufmann were camped high above Moraine Lake with intentions of climbing either Deltaform Mtn. or Mt. Hungabee. However, unstable snow conditions precluded either attempt so they settled on a first ascent of Neptuak Mtn. Wooley stated:

Deltaform and Neptuak Mtns. loom over the shoulder of Eiffel Pk.

*It was good hard scrambling nearly the whole way, the rocks being almost vertical in places and the hand-holds not over-abundant; and, being a party of five on one rope, we made slow progress. Towards the summit the inevitable cornice was encountered, and, travers-ing some distance below it, we climbed a narrow ridge of rocks overhung with snow and found ourselves on the highest point at 3 p.m.*

Stutfield and Collie, 1903

## Wenkchemna Pk. 3173 m

Samuel Allen applied this name to the 10th peak in the valley surround-ing Moraine Lake. It is the only one not visible from Moraine Lake and it is unclear to which peak Allen was actually referring.

## The Wenkchemna Puzzle

The entire issue surrounding Allen's original Ten Peaks is quite confusing. Peak #10 (Wenkchemna) is really nothing more than a minor shoulder of the much more impressive mountain Allen named Hungabee. Allen's map clearly shows both of these mountains to be separate and distinct peaks. Being hard to iden-tify, not visible from Moraine Lake, and separated from the other major peaks in the valley only adds to the confusion. These facts led Hugh Stutfield, J. Norman Collie, and J.W.A. Dickson to speculate that Allen was actually referring to Mt. Hungabee as Peak #10. Others be-lieve that Mt. Babel was actually Allen's Peak #1, which would make more sense. Or, perhaps Allen's fad-ing memory and bouts with schizo-phrenia simply placed Peak #10 on the wrong side of Wenkchemna Pass.

# Consolation Valley

Another gem of the Canadian Rockies remained hidden un-til Walter Wilcox and Ross Peacock brought it to attention in 1899. On August 19 they were follow-ing a stream coming in from the southeast, below Moraine Lake when "suddenly a long stretch of wa-ter opened before us and disclosed a beautiful scene. Beyond the pretty banks of the stream, lined with birch and willow bushes, appeared in the distance an Alpine peak, fringed in a narrow border of ice near its tooth-like crest …" Wilcox was describing the four distinct pinnacles that form the summit of Mt. Quadra at the head of the valley and the scene so contrasted with the utter desolation of the adjacent valley that, upon Ross's suggestion, he was compelled to name it Consolation Valley. Wilcox was so enamoured with its beauty that he continued, saying it com-bined "every element of grandeur and beauty characteristic of the Canadian Rockies – vertical cliffs and glaciers, forests, meadows, and a water surface, the reflections in which give an added interest to the surroundings."

Mt. Babel over
Consolation Lake

# The Consolation Peaks

## Panorama Ridge
## 2800 m

The name is descriptive, referring to the fabulous views obtained from the summit of the ridge. The Bow Valley, as well as Consolation Lakes and the peaks surrounding the lakes, are revealed in a 360° panorama. In the autumn, when the larch needles turn golden, the entire ridge appears set aglow and the hike to the lakes is a distinct alternative to always overcrowded Larch Valley.

## The Legend of Lyall's
## Larch

Lyall's larch is a subalpine tree species that has the distinction of being the only conifer to lose its needles in the fall. However, before losing its needles the tree puts on a brilliant autumn display as the green chlorophyll pigments are gradually replaced by the vivid yellow and orange carotenoid pigments. The species name honours Scottish botanist and surgeon David Lyall (1817 – 1895) who collected many specimens while serving for the North American Boundary

Panorama Ridge
from Outlet Creek
viewpoint

Commission. Why does Lyall's larch lose its needles in the fall? An old native legend (adapted here from *Old Man's Garden* by Annora Brown) accounts for this peculiarity in the botanical world.

> Long ago the Indians could talk to the trees in a language they both could understand. As the great old chiefs of the Indians died the trees continued to grow and thrive but this ability to communicate was gradually lost. The trees continued to communicate with each other in whispered conversations, which the Indians no longer understood and The Great Spirit called a conference of the forest trees in an attempt to remedy this situation. At this conference the trees were required to remain awake for seven days and nights. Some of the trees remained faithfully awake to the end while others found the task too strenuous and fell asleep. The larch tree was one of the weaker mem-

> bers at this council and fell asleep. This greatly angered the Great Spirit who punished the weaker members by compelling them to lose their protective coats in the fall. They were forced to suffer through the icy blasts of winter without their clothes. However, the benevolent Great Spirit promised that each spring their hair would be given back to them. And that is how the larch trees came to lose their needles in the fall.

## Mt. Babel 3101 m and the Tower of Babel 2360 m

Looming above Moraine Lake is a monolithic tower composed of quartzite that is part of Mt. Babel. "Babel" is composed of two words; "baa" meaning "gate" and "el" meaning "god," hence, "the gate of god." The tower must have reminded Wilcox of Genesis 11, "Come let us build ourselves a city, and a tower with its top in the heavens ..."

because that is the name he ascribed to the tower that has its top in the heavens and acts as the gateway to heavenly Moraine Lake and the Valley of the Ten Peaks.

## A New Use for Toilet Paper!

The east face of Mt. Babel has been an object of interest to climbers for many years. In 1996 it was the scene of a rescue in which Walter Perren would test his recently designed winch and pulley system for mountain rescue. Two young, experienced climbers, Brian Greenwood and Charlie Locke, were attempting the first ascent of the awesome northeast face of Mt. Babel when they encountered a 'minor problem." The following account of their ordeal has been adapted from *The Mountaineers* by Phil Dowling.

Greenwood and Locke arose from their second bivouac spent on a stony platform, no more than a metre square and prepared to tackle

the final overhanging 75-m face that led to the summit. Greenwood led as far as a rock roof at which point Locke took over the lead, driving pitons into the rock and held in place only by Greenwood's belay and the stirrups under his feet.

One by one Locke managed to drive pitons into the overhanging wall, hook a stirrup in place, and then pull himself upwards. It took Locke one hour to place five pitons. As he pulled himself up to the last and highest piton, it came out! Locke found himself falling backwards off the wall as one by one the pitons he had so laboriously worked to place were jerked free from the rock. Locke plunged 15 m backwards into space before Greenwood's belay and the last piton brought his fall to a jolting arrest. "Snarled and tangled in his gear; the fallen climber righted himself painfully and examined the damage. His left hand, where the weight of his body had struck the rock, was connected to his forearm by two right-angled bends. With his

**Left: Subalpine larch in autumn**

**Right: Panorama Ridge from Baker Creek**

Mt. Babel

Tower of Babel

Tower of Babel

good right arm Locke managed to regain the ledge; then he started to pass out."

Greenwood was in a quandry; what to do next? Descent was out of the question and he couldn't leave Locke alone for fear of tumbling off the face. To make matters worse, they had consumed all of their water and the only food they had left was a small amount of butter. Worse, Greenwood was nearly out of cigarettes! So, securing each other to the small ledge they began to yell in the hope that someone in the valley below would hear them. As luck would have it, two climbers heard their cries of anguish and immediately went for help.

When Walter Perren arrived at the scene he quickly assessed that rescue from below was impossible and would have to be attempted from above, by helicopter. The problem was that the only available helicopter was in Jasper and wouldn't be available until late that evening. It was then that Walter sent Warden Jay Morton back to Moraine Lake for a

Bident Mtn.  Mt. Quadra  Mt. Babel

roll of toilet paper. Yes, toilet paper! On it Walter scrolled the message "WAIT HELP COMING TOP AM." Then he rolled it out on the ground below the stranded climbers who read it from their perch high above. It would be another cold night stranded on the face of the mountain.

The next morning all equipment had been assembled and ferried to the summit ridge. Bill Vrcom was selected to descend the wall, attached only to a wire cable anchored to a pulley system on the ridge. He would be the first to test this system designed by Perren for rescue from just such impossible places. First Locke and then Greenwood were hoisted to the ridge in a Gramminger rescue seat on the back of Warden Bill Vroom. By 2:00 p.m. the rescue was complete. It marked the first use of the block-and-tackle system devised by Perren and the first time a helicopter had been used in a Rocky Mountain rescue. Thus ended Greenwood and Locke's first attempt of the east face of Babel. "Later he

[Greenwood] would laconically state; it was just as well, really. As it turned out we were going the wrong way."

## Mt. Quadra 3173 m

Mt. Quadra is a spectacular mountain at the head of Consolation Valley that was named by A.O. Wheeler because of its four distinct rocky pinnacles. When I look at the peak it reminds me of four teeth with huge gaps obviously in need of a good orthodontist!

## Bident Mtn. 3084 m

Bident Mtn., also at the head of Consolation Valley is another "toothy" peak. Located just east of Mt. Quadra, it was named because of its two gigantic, tooth-like towers. In 1903 C.S. Thompson and guide Hans Kaufmann made the first ascent of the mountain.

Opposite top: Spectacular view of Mt. Babel and the Tower of Babel from the Panorama Ridge trail

Opposite bottom: The Tower of Babel from the Rockpile

Above: Looking into Consolation Valley from the road to Moraine Lake

# Kicking Horse Pass

Waputik Icefield

Mt. Hector

Eastern approach to Kicking Horse Pass from the summit of Mt. St. Piran. The Icefield Parkway separates the Waputik Icefield from Mt. Hector

*We were lucky in finding an old Stony Indian who drew a map for us on birch bark that proved to be an invaluable aid in our search for a pass. This later proved to be near where the doctor met the serious acci-dent with his saddle horse. When we were through the pass he predicted that some day it would be the route of a railway.*

Peter Erasmus

# A Fortuitous Wink!

It is only fitting that we end our journey with another legend about the remarkable James Hector. After crossing Vermilion Pass he continued his journey down the Vermilion River to Kootenay Crossing, following the aforementioned map the old Stoney had drawn. At Kootenay Crossing he turned northwest and followed the Kootenay River to its headwaters from where he then followed the Beaverfoot River to its junction with the Kicking Horse River. At Wapta Falls, where the two rivers meet, one of the most famous events in the history of the exploration of the Rocky Mountains took place.

On August 29, 1858, Hector's party had just emerged from a torturous journey from the headwaters of the Beaverfoot River. At its junction with another large river Hector noted:

> Here we met a very large stream, equal in size to the Bow River where we crossed it. This river descends the valley from the north-west, and, on entering the wide valley of Beaverfoot River, turns back on its course at a sharp angle, receives that river as its tributary, and flows off to the south-west through the other valley. Just above the angle there is a fall about 40 feet in height, where the channel is contracted by perpendicular rocks.

Hector had reached present-day Wapta Falls and was now about to attempt to return east to the Bow River drainage across the Great Divide using an ancient route. It is here that the historic event took place. Hector continued:

> A little way above this fall, one of our pack horses, to escape the fallen timber, plunged into the stream luckily where it formed an eddy, but the banks were so steep that we had great difficulty in getting him out. In attempting to catch my own horse, which had strayed off while we were engaged with the one in the water, he kicked

me in the chest, but I had luckily got close to him before he struck out, so that I did not get the full force of the blow.

The force of the blow knocked Hector unconscious and what followed were stories that are part fact, part myth, and part legend. Hector insisted that the blow only "rendered me senseless for some time," but Peter Erasmus seemed to recall a much more serious event and remembered Hector being rendered unconscious for at least two hours. The men had given up hope of Hector's recovery at which point, unable to detect any signs of life, they prepared to bury him. According to Erasmus, it was at this juncture that Hector regained consciousness and, "still unable to speak, he managed to wink, so saving himself from untimely interment." The Kicking Horse River and Pass were both named in memory of this historic event.

James Hector continued his epic journey across Bow Pass and then to Howse Pass, which David Thompson discovered in 1807. Turning his back on the mountains, he made his way to Fort Edmonton. His journey, which started at Old Bow Fort on August 11, 1858, finally ended when he entered Fort Edmonton on October 7. He had been on the trail for 58 days and covered over 800 km of wild, unmapped territory.

# A Twist of Fate

In 1861 James Hector was appointed the director of the Geological Survey of Otago, New Zealand. Here he would spend the next 40 years of his life exploring the natural resources of this distant land. By the time he retired in 1903 he was in poor health, his body showing the effects of the hardship and punishment it was forced to endure during his explorations.

But, one thing remained, an

abiding desire to return to the site of his youthful accomplishments and the Kicking Horse Pass. In 1903, the Canadian Pacific Railway set in motion a grandiose scheme for a triumphant return of the intrepid explorer. He arrived in Vancouver on July 12 full of excitement accompanied by his youngest son Douglas. Things had changed drastically since his last visit causing Hector to comment that he "felt like a perfect Rip Van Winkle." When he stepped off the train at Glacier Station, the man whose name alone invoked a deep and abiding reverence was welcomed by a younger generation of climbers, explorers and visitors full of curiosity. Little did they know writes Mary Schäffer; "...when the snowy-haired traveller descended from the train at Glacier, that hopes were to go unrealized, and that he would return alone with his sorrow to his home, leaving a young, bright son, to rest forever in the valley of the Columbia."

**James Hector, circa 1856 courtesy of James Donald Hector, his great grandson**

Hector spent his first evening spinning tales of that famous expedition to his excited and eager listeners. Mary Schäffer recounts that, slapping his knee emphatically Hector blurted, "There is one place I mean to see, and that's my grave!" "Your grave?" someone asked. "Yes," Hector continued, "I'm sure I can go to the exact spot." After recounting the famous incident Hector amusingly commented, "... I did not use that grave. Instead, they named the river the Kicking Horse, and gave the Pass, which we made our way through a few days later, the same name."

Alas, Hector did not get a chance to return to see the marvelous bit of engineering that had been constructed through his pass; his son suddenly become very ill. As his condition rapidly grew worse it was decided to move him to Revelstoke Hospital, where 36 hours later he died from an acute attack of appendicitis. Mary Schäffer writes that those that gathered around the gravesite grieved not only for the one that was gone, but also for "...the one that was left. Where the Selkirk Mountains will forever cast their purple shadows across his grave, where the winding Columbia will murmur a dirge as long as the river flows, we left him." A headstone carved from the same granite as that used to construct the monument placed on the Continental Divide to commemorate his father's achievement was erected to mark Douglas' grave.

Unexpectedly, one of those present at the funeral happened to be Sir Edward Whymper. The two famous men had never met, but they had known of each other's accomplishments for many years. Mary Schäffer states that, "The first handclasp of the two well-known men was one worth seeing." This once in a lifetime occasion was punctuated by Hector uttering a simple yet momentous phrase in recognition of the conqueror of the Matterhorn, "Ah Whymper, is it you?"

The pain of his son's death was more than an aging Sir James could endure. He returned to New Zealand at once, a broken man. Three years later he died at the age of 74, survived by his widow, two remaining sons, and three daughters. In 1903 Mary Schäffer wrote, 'It seems strange that a man who struck such a superb blow for the liberation of the west from its vast solitude, silence and impassibility, should be so little known today among general travelers." Sadly, the same may be said of today's travellers because, "such men as he are few."

# The Canadian Pacific Railway

The difficult terrain on the western slopes of Kicking Horse Pass made it a poor choice for the transcontinental line but it was the shortest route to the Pacific. By the winter of 1883 the track had reached the summit of Kicking Horse Pass and the following year it crossed the pass. Hector had been very prophetic when he predicted that someday the pass would be a route for a rail line!

Just west of Revelstoke, B.C., at Craigellachie, on November 7, 1885, on a cold and dreary day, Donald Smith drove the "last spike" and Prime Minister John A. Macdonald's "national dream' of a railway line from coast to coast was no longer a dream. It had taken 14 troublesome years to complete but in achieving the impossible the future of a fledgling nation had been secured.

A few months later, the "Architect of Confederation," Sir John A. Macdonald, and his wife Lady Agnes, would celebrate this historic event by taking the train across the Dominion of Canada. At Laggan, Lady Agnes insisted on riding the locomotive's cowcatcher and her account of this thrilling ride at the front of the locomotive in a makeshift seat provides a fitting ending to this story. Enthroned on the cowcatcher seat and wrapped in a linen carriage-cover, she described the experience for *Murray's Magazine*" as "a thrill that is very like fear; but it is gone at once and I can think of nothing but the novelty, the excitement, and the fun of this mad ride in glorious sunshine and intoxicating air, with magnificent mountains before and around me."

# Chronology

**10,000 B.C:** Early human occupation on the shores of Lake Minnewanka and Vermilion Lakes.

**1700s:** The Stoneys migrate to the Rocky Mountains.

**1754:** Anthony Henday may have viewed "The Shining Mountains."

**1800:** David Thompson and Duncan McGillivray explore the Bow Valley as far as Lac des Arcs.

**1807:** David Thompson crosses Howse Pass.

**1841:** Sir George Simpson and James Sinclair pass through the Lake Minnewanka region. Simpson discovers Simpson Pass; Sinclair discovers White Man Pass.

**1845:** Father de Smet and British soldiers Henry Warre and Mervin Vavasour cross White Man Pass.

**1847:** Reverend Robert Terrill Rundle visits the region.

**1850:** James Sinclair makes a second crossing of White Man Pass.

**1854:** Sinclair leads another group of settlers across North Kananaskis Pass to the Oregon Territory.

**1858:** Captain John Palliser crosses North Kananaskis Pass.

**1858:** Sir James Hector of the Palliser Expedition explores the Bow Valley and discovers Vermilion Pass, Kicking Horse Pass, and Bow Pass. Hector names many of the mountains in the area.

**1859:** Hector returns and journeys up the Bow Valley, discovers Pipestone Pass, and crosses Howse Pass to the Columbia River.

**1859:** The Earl of Southesk becomes the first tourist to visit what is now Jasper National Park, returning across Pipestone Pass and the Bow River Valley.

**1881:** CPR chooses Kicking Horse Pass as its route through the Rocky Mountains.

**1881–1884:** The Geological Survey of Canada (under the stewardship of Dr. George Mercer Dawson and with the assistance of Richard McConnell), begins mapping the southern and central Rocky Mountains.

**1882:** Stoney guide Edwin Hunter guides Tom Wilson to Lake Louise.

**1883:** CPR reaches Siding 29 (now Banff) and Laggan (now Lake Louise).

**1883:** Silver City becomes a boom town.

**1883:** William McCardell, Thomas McCardell, and Frank McCabe "discover" the hot springs at the Cave and Basin.

**1884:** The CPR main line crosses Kicking Horse Pass.

**1885:** The Hot Springs Reserve is created.

**1885:** The "last spike" is driven at Craigellachie, just west of Revelstoke B.C., marking the completion of the transcontinental railway line.

**1886:** George Stewart creates an infrastructure that would make the Hot Springs Reserve a credible park. Banff officially becomes a town.

**1886:** Prime Minister Sir John A. Macdonald and Lady Agnes visit the Rockies.

**1886-89:** James J. McArthur completes topographic work of the mountains along the CPR main line for the Government of Canada.

**1887:** The Hot Springs Reserve is increased in size and becomes Rocky Mountains National Park.

**1887:** The Vaux Family visits the Selkirk Mountains and the Rocky Mountains.

**1888:** Reverend Spotswood Green visits Lake Louise.

**1888:** The original log-framed building Banff Springs Hotel is constructed.

**1890:** The first "Chalet" is built on the shores of Lake Louise by the CPR.

**1891:** Samuel E.S. Allen makes a short visit to Lake Louise.

**1892:** The area around Lake Louise is added to Rocky Mountains National Park.

**1893:** Samuel Allen and Walter Wilcox explore the Lake Louise region.

**1894:** The Yale Club explores and names most of the landmarks in the Lake Louise, Paradise Valley, and Moraine Lake regions.

**1896:** Philip S. Abbot becomes the first climbing casualty in the Rocky Mountains.

**1897:** Swiss guide Peter Sarbach leads successful attempts on Mts. Lefroy and Victoria.

**1899:** Walter Wilcox and Ross Peacock become the first visitors to Moraine and Consolation Lakes.

**1899:** Swiss guides Edward Feuz Sr. and Christian Easler Sr. are brought to Canada by the CPR.

**1900:** Bill and Jim Brewster begin outfitting and guiding in Banff.

**1900:** CPR constructs the mining town of Bankhead.

**1901:** World-renowned climber Edward Whymper arrives in the Rockies.

**1903:** Swiss guide Edward Feuz Jr. arrives in the Rockies.

**1906:** The Alpine Club of Canada is formed under the leadership of A.O. Wheeler.

**1909:** Conrad Kain arrives from Austria to begin his remarkable guiding career in the Rockies.

**1909:** Ernest Feuz and Rudolph Aemmer begin guiding in the Rockies.

**1911:** The Banff Coach Road is constructed.

**1912:** Walter Feuz begins guiding in the Rockies.

**1913–1927:** The Boundary Commission, under the leadership of A.O. Wheeler and Richard Cautley, begins its monumental work.

**1915:** Prisoner of War camp constructed at Castle Mtn.

**1921:** The road between Banff and Lake Louise is completed.

**1923:** The Banff/Windermere Highway is opened.

**1924:** Fire destroys the Chalet at Lake Louise.

**1925:** Reconstruction of the Chalet at Lake Louise is completed and opens under the name Chateau Lake Louise.

**1926:** Fire destroys the north wing of The Banff Springs Hotel.

**1928:** Reconstruction of The Banff Springs Hotel is completed, essentially as it looks today.

**1930:** The National Parks Act is passed by Parliament, establishing the boundaries of the park much as they exist today. Rocky Mountains Park is renamed Banff National Park.

**1950:** Walter Perren becomes the last Swiss guide in Canada, after which he joins the National Park Warden Service and develops modern rescue methods.

**1962:** The Trans-Canada Highway is officially opened.

**1990:** Banff becomes a self-governing municipality within the Province of Alberta.

# References

Abbot, Philip S. "The First Ascent of Mt. Hector." *Appalachia,* vol. 8 (1896).

Allen, S.E.S. "Mountaineering in the Canadian Rockies." *The Alpine Journal,* vol. 18 (1896 – 97).

Allen, S.E.S. *Explorations among the Watershed Rockies of Canada.* Ottawa: Canadian Institute for Historical Microreproductions, 1980.

Anderson, Frank W. *Enchanted Banff and Lake Louise.* Calgary: Frontier Publishing, 1968.

Beers, Don. *The World of Lake Louise: A Guide for Hikers.* Calgary: Highline Publishing, 1991.

Bella, Leslie. *Parks for Profit.* Montreal: Harvest House, 1987.

Belyea, Barbara, ed. *David Thompson's Columbia Journals.* Montreal: McGill-Queen's University Press, 1994.

Berton, Pierre. *The Last Spike.* Toronto: McClelland and Stewart, 1971.

Birney, Earle. *The Collected Poems of Earle Birney.* Toronto: McClelland and Stewart Ltd., 1975.

Boles, Glen W., Roberta Kruszyna, and William L. Putnam. *The Rocky Mountains of Canada South.* New York: The American Alpine Club; Banff: The Alpine Club of Canada, 1979.

Brown, Annora. *Old Man's Garden.* Sidney, B.C.: Gray's Publishing, 1970.

Brown, Robert Craig. "The Doctrine of Usefulness: Natural Resources and National Park Policy in Canada, 1887 – 1914." In *The Canadian National Parks Today and Tomorrow,* edited by J.G. Nelson. Calgary: University of Calgary Press, 1968.

Burnett, R.I.M. "The life and work of sir James Hector. With special reference to the Hector Collection." Unpublished M.A. Thesis, University of Otago, New Zealand, 1936.

Canada. Department of the Interior. *Annual Report for 1903.*

Canada. Commission Appointed to Delimit the Boundary between the Provinces of Alberta and British Columbia. *Report of the Commission Appointed to Delimit the Boundary between the Provinces of Alberta and British Columbia, Part I, from 1913 to 1916.* [Ottawa]: Office of the Surveyor General, 1917. Commission co-chairs were R.W. Cautley, J.N. Wallace, and A.O. Wheeler.

Canada. House of Commons. *Debates,* April 10, 1930, no. 1454.

Chumak, Sebastian. *The Stonies of Alberta: an illustrated heritage of genesis, myths, legends, folklore, and wisdom of Yahey Wichastabi.* Narrated by 12 Stoney Elders; Translated by Alfred "Toots" Dixon; recorded by Thomas T. Williams. Calgary: The Alberta Foundation, 1983.

Clark, Ella E. *Indian Legends from the Northern Rockies.* Norman: University of Oklahoma Press, 1966.

Coleman, A.P. *The Canadian Rockies: New and Old Trails.* Toronto: Henry Frowde, 1911.

Collie, Norman J., and Hugh Stutfield. *Climbs and Explorations in the Canadian Rockies.* London: Longman, Green, 1903.

De Smet, Father Pierre. *Oregon Missions and Travels over the Rocky Mountains in 1845-46.* New York: Edward Dunigan, 1847.

Dempsey, Hugh (ed). *The Rundle Journals, 1840-1848.* Calgary: Historical Society of Alberta and Glenbow-Alberta Institute, 1977.

Dempsey, Hugh A. *Indians of the Rocky Mountain Parks*. Calgary: Fifth House, 1998.

Dempsey, Hugh A., ed "David Thompson's Journey to the Red Deer River." *Alberta Historical Review*, vol. 13 (1965).

Dixon, Harold B. "The Ascent of Mt. Lefroy, and Other Climbs in the Rocky Mountains." *The Alpine Journal*, vol. 19 (1898).

Dowling, Phil. *The Mountaineers*. Edmonton: Hurtig, 1979.

Erasmus, Peter, as told to Henry Thompson. *Buffalo Days and Night*. Calgary: Fifth House, 1990.

Fay, Charles E. "The First Ascent of Mt. Victoria." *Appalachia*, vol. 10 (1899).

Fay, Charles E. "Old Times in the Canadian Alps." *Canadian Alpine Journal*, vol. 12 (1922).

Fleming, Sandford. *England and Canada, A Summer Tour between Old and New Westminster*. London: Sampson, Low, Marston, Searle and Rivington, 1884.

Fraser, Esther. *The Canadian Rockies*. Edmonton: Hurtig, 1969.

Gadd, Ben. *Bankhead, The Twenty Year Town*. The Friends of Banff National Park, 1989.Green, Harry. "Tragedy on Mt. Victoria." *Canadian Alpine Journal*, vol. 38 (1955).

Green, William Spotswood. *Among the Selkirk Glaciers*. London: Macmillan, 1890.

Hart, E.J. *Diamond Hitch*. Banff: Summerthought, 1979.

Hart, E.J. *The Place of Bows*. Banff: EJH Literary Enterprises, 1999.

Henday, Anthony. *A Year Inland: The Journal of a Hudson's Bay Company Winterer*. Edited by Barbara Belyea. Waterloo: Wilfred Laurier University Press, 2000.

Henderson, Yandell. "The Summer of 1894 around Lake Louise." *Canadian Alpine Journal*, vol. 22 (1933).

Hickson, J.W.A. "The Ascent of Pinnacle Mountain and Second Ascent of Mount Deltaform." *Canadian Alpine Journal*, vol. 2 (1910).

Kauffman, Andrew, and William L. Putnam. *The Guiding Spirit*. Revelstoke: Footprint Publishing, 1986.

Lent, D. Geneva. *West of the Mountains: James Sinclair and the Hudson's Bay Co*. Seattle: University of Washington Press, 1963.

Luxton, Eleanor G. *Banff Canada's First National Park* Banff: Summerthought Ltd., 1975.

MacCarthy, A.H. "The First Ascent of Mt. Louis." *Canadian Alpine Journal*, vol. 8 (1917).

MacEwan, Grant. *Fifty Mighty Men*. Saskatoon: Western Producer Prairie Books, 1982.

MacGregor, James. G. *Behold the Shining Mountains: Being an Account of the Travels of Anthony Henday, 1745 – 55, the First White Man To Enter Alberta*. Edmonton: Applied Art Products, 1954.

McCardell, William. "Reminiscences of a Western Pioneer." Whyte Museum of the Canadian Rockies Archives.

Outram, James. *In the Heart of the Canadian Rockies*. London and New York: Macmillan, 1906.

Parker, Elizabeth. "Edward Whymper Obituary." *Canadian Alpine Journal*, vol. 4 (1912).

Parker, Herschel C. "The Ascent of Mt. Hungabee." *Canadian Alpine Journal*, vol. 1, 19, (1907).

Pearce, William. "Establishment of National Parks in the Rockies." *Alberta Historical Review*, vol. 10 (1962).

Sandford, R.W. *The Canadian Alps*. Banff: Altitude Publishing, 1990.

Scace, Robert C. *Banff: A Cultural—Historical Study of Land Use and Management in a National Park Community to 1945*. Masters thesis, University of Calgary, 1968.

Schäffer, Mary, "Sir James Hector," *Rod and Gun in Canada*, January, 1904.

Simpson. George. *Narrative of a Journey round the World during the Years 1841 and 1842*. London: Henry Colburn, 1847.

Smith, Cyndi. *Off the Beaten Track*. Lake Louise: Coyote Books, 1989.

Snow, Chief John. *These Mountains Are Our Sacred Places*. Toronto: S. Stevens, 1977.

Spry, Irene. *The Palliser Papers, 1857 – 60*. Toronto: Champlain Society, 1968.

Stutfield, H.E.M., and Norman J. Collie. *Climbs and Explorations in the Canadian Rockies*. London: Longman, Green, 1903.

Thomas. A. "How Banff Got Its Name," *Crag and Canyon*, (reprinted from the Vancouver Province). October 27, 1939.

Thompson, Charles S. "The Coulier on Mount Lefroy." *Appalachia*, vol. 8 (1896).

Thomson, Theresa A. "One Thousand Climbs to Breakfast." *Alberta Historical Review*, vol. 10 (1962).

Tyrrell, J.B., ed. *David Thompson: Narratives of His Explorations in Western North America, 1784 – 1812*. Toronto: Champlain Society, 1916.

Waiser, Bill. *Park Prisoners: The Untold Story of Western Canada's National Parks, 1915 – 1946*. Saskatoon and Calgary: Fifth House, 1995

Warre, H.J. *Overland to Oregon in 1845: Impressions of a Journey across North America*. Ottawa: Public Archives of Canada, 1976.

Whyte, Jon, and Carole Harmon. *Lake Louise: A Diamond in the Wilderness*. Banff: Altitude Publishing, 1982.

Wilcox, Walter D. *Camping in the Canadian Rockies*. New York: G.P. Putman's Sons, 1897.

Wilcox, Walter D. *The Rockies of Canada*. New York: Knickerbocker Press, 1916.

Williams, Mabel .B. *Guardians of the Wild*. New York: Thomas Nelson and Sons, 1936.

Wilson, Thomas E., as told to W.E. Round. *Trail Blazer of the Canadian Rockies*. Edited by Hugh A. Dempsey. Calgary: Glenbow – Alberta Institute, 1972.

# Index

# Index

# Index

# Photographic Credits

**Banff Park Museum**
Permission to photograph the Simpson tree trunk (p.66)

**Canadian Pacific Railway**
p.108 (NS 85)

**Glenbow Museum**
front cover (NA 4868-197), p.16 (NA 1252-3), p.21(left) (NA 637-6), p.22(left) (NA 339-1), back cover & p.27 (NC 26-196), p.28 (NA 1539-1), p.31 (NA 1949-1), p.32 (NA 573-4), p.35(top) (NA 717-9), p. 35(bottom) & p.69(bottom) (NA 1188-1), p.41 left) (NA 7-175), p.43 (NA 5258-17), p.44(left) (NA 2943-1), p.44(right) (NA 1658-1), p.45(bottom) (NA 714-260), p.51 (NA 2371-1), p.53(top) (NA 1391-1), p.74 (NA 553-1), p.75 (NA 1870-7), p.76(top) (NA 1870-18), p.84(bottom) (NA 699-1), p.85(bottom) (NA 345-29), 87(bottom) (NA 2451-12), p.89 (NA 673-21), 91(top) (NA 1804-1), p.91(bottom) (NA 937-9), p.98 (NA 4868-184), p.107 (bottom right) (NA 673-19), p.135(bottom) (NA 2615-1).

**Carole Harmon**
p.33, p.141.

**Don Harmon**
p.97(bottom)

**James Donald Hector**
p.148

**Stephen Hutchings**
p.114, p.131, p.144(top).

**National Archives of Canada**
p.15 (C-009190), p.22(right) (C 149942), p.30 (PA 26439), p.36(top) (PA 182603), p.40(right) (C 20607), p.50(bottom) (C 044702), p.52 (C 040850), p.54 (PA 023141), p.55(bottom) (PA 025699), p.56 (right) (PA 149332), p.58 (PA 58181), p.63(bottom) (PA 42946), p.64(left) (PA 027869), p.73(top) (PA 171942), p.82(bottom) (C 22832), p.88 (PA 28729), p.90 (PA 11031), p.94(right) (PA 203034), p. 96 (PA 673-11), p.100 (C 009313), p.104(left) (PA 025322), p.105(bottom) (PA 027050), p.123(top) (PA 027335), p.123(bottom) (PA 025809).

**Parks Canada**
p. 18 Chamber of Jewels painting by Dan Frache.

**Saskatchewan Archives Board**
p. 68(bottom) (RA 4982)

**Dennis Schmidt**
p.77, p.111(bottom right)

**Roger Schmidt**
p.103 (3-612), p.105 (6-161), p.107 (6-162), p.112 (3-609), p.113 (5-270), p.128 (5-276), p.127(top) (5-243), p.129(bottom) (5-275), p.132 (5-248), p.134 (5-249), p.136 (5-227), p.138 (5-226), p.139 (5-263), p.146 (6-172).

**TransAlta Corporation**
p.46, p.49.

**Whyte Museum of the Canadian Rockies**
p.8 (V527 NG-124), p.21(bottom) (V412/LC), p.41(right) (NA 66-58), p.42(bottom) (NA 66-325), p.62 (NA 66-408), p.67(bottom) (PA 240-1), p.95 (NA 66-1981), p.97(top) (VC701/LC10), p.101 (NA 66-1990), p.117 (NA 66-2251), p.121 (NA 66-2268) p.133(bottom) (V14 ACOP802), p.134(bottom) (NA 66-254).

**Yale University**
p.119(top) (Y671-893), p.119(bottom) (Y671-895), p.137 (RU 684).

# About the Author

Ernie Lakusta's interests have always been science and the mountains. Majoring in the biological sciences, Ernie graduated with a B. Ed. degree in 1966 and a M. Sc. degree in 1970. His research was based in Kananaskis Country and it was during this period that he became an avid hiker, amateur photographer, and self-taught naturalist.

To this day, the mountains are his passion and he avails himself of every opportunity to travel off the beaten track with his wife Jean and family members. He is also the author of *Canmore & Kananaskis History Explorer.* Ernie lives in Calgary.